Praise for Joan Didion's

Miami

"With customary flair, Didion ignores the traditional features of Miami, looks briefly at tense race relations, white flight, and a saturated real-estate market, and concentrates on a kind of second city, the community of Cuban exiles who have prospered even as they pursue *la lucha*, the struggle. . . . Didion presents a more complex and genuinely dramatic situation . . . lingering on the kinds of details that have colored her other writings: a hotel offering 'guerrilla discounts,' a gun shop advertising Father's Day specials, a house blessed with 'Unusual Security and Ready Access to the Ocean.' *Miami* is another persistently stylish report that, with its JFK references and drug-runner allusions, has even more outreach than usual."
—*Kirkus Reviews*

"Joan Didion's *Miami* is a prose voyage through the world of Cuban Florida, a trip of discovery that only the author of *Slouching Towards Bethlehem, The White Album,* and *Salvador* could take us on."
— *Vogue*

"Didion's competitors in the field do not even approach her in sophistication, analytic precision, and stylistic grace. . . . Didion's *Miami*, like her *Salvador*, is a thoroughly researched and brilliantly written meditation on the consequences of power. . . ."
—*The Village Voice Literary Supplement*

AN EDITOR'S CHOICE SELECTION OF
THE NEW YORK TIMES
AND *TIME* MAGAZINE

Books by Joan Didion

Run River*
Slouching Towards Bethlehem*
Play It as It Lays*
A Book of Common Prayer*
The White Album*
Salvador*
Democracy*
Miami**

*Published by WASHINGTON SQUARE PRESS
**Published by POCKET BOOKS

Joan Didion

Miami

POCKET BOOKS

New York   London   Toronto   Sydney   Tokyo

Excerpts from this book have appeared in *The New York Review of Books* in slightly different form.

POCKET BOOKS, a division of Simon & Schuster Inc.
1230 Avenue of the Americas, New York, N.Y. 10020

ISBN: 0-671-66820-X

First Pocket Books trade paperback printing September, 1988

10 9 8 7 6 5 4 3 2 1

POCKET and colophon are trademarks
of Simon & Schuster Inc.

Printed in the U.S.A.

This book is for
Eduene Jerrett Didion
and
Frank Reese Didion

ONE

1

HAVANA vanities come to dust in Miami. On the August night in 1933 when General Gerardo Machado, then president of Cuba, flew out of Havana into exile, he took with him five revolvers, seven bags of gold, and five friends, still in their pajamas. Gerardo Machado is buried now in a marble crypt at Woodlawn Park Cemetery in Miami, Section Fourteen, the mausoleum. On the March night in 1952 when Carlos Prío Socarrás, who had helped depose Gerardo Machado in 1933 and had fifteen years later become president himself, flew out of Havana into exile, he took with him his foreign minister, his minister of the interior, his wife and his two small daughters. A photograph of the occasion shows Señora de Prío, quite beautiful, boarding the plane in what appears to be a raw silk suit, and a hat with black fishnet veiling. She wears gloves, and earrings. Her makeup is fresh. The husband and father, recently the president, wears dark glasses, and carries the younger child, María Elena, in his arms.

Carlos Prío is now buried himself at Woodlawn Park Cemetery in Miami, Section Three, not far from Gerardo Machado, in a grave marked by a six-foot marble stone on which the flag of Cuba waves in red, white and blue ceramic tile. CARLOS PRÍO SOCARRÁS 1903–1977, the stone reads, and directly below that, as if Carlos Prío Socarrás's main hedge against oblivion had been that period at the University of Havana when he was running actions against Gerardo Machado: MIEMBRO DEL DIRECTORIO ESTUDIANTIL UNIVERSITARIO 1930. Only then does the legend PRESIDENTE DE LA REPÚBLICA DE CUBA 1948–1952 appear, an anticlimax. Presidencies are short and the glamours of action long, there among the fallen frangipani and crepe myrtle blossoms at Woodlawn Park Cemetery in Miami. "They say that I was a terrible president of Cuba," Carlos Prío once said to Arthur M. Schlesinger, Jr., during a visit to the Kennedy White House some ten years into the quarter-century Miami epilogue to his four-year Havana presidency. "That may be true. But I was the best president Cuba ever had."

Many Havana epilogues have been played in Florida, and some prologues. Florida is that part of the Cuban stage where declamatory exits are made, and side deals. Florida is where the chorus waits to comment on the action, and sometimes to join it. The exiled José Martí raised money among the Cuban tobacco workers in Key West and Tampa, and in 1894 attempted to mount an invasionary expedition from north of Jacksonville. The exiled Fidel Castro Ruz came to Miami in 1955 for money to take the 26 Julio into the Sierra Maestra, and got it, from Carlos Prío. Fulgencio Batista had himself come back from Florida to take Havana away from Carlos Prío in 1952, but by 1958 Fidel Castro, with Carlos Prío's money, was taking it away from Fulgencio Batista, at which turn Carlos Prío's former prime minister tried to land a third force in Camagüey Province, the idea being to seize the moment from Fidel Castro, a notably failed undertaking encouraged by the Central Intelligence Agency and financed by Carlos Prío, at home in Miami Beach.

This is all instructive. In the continuing opera still called, even by Cubans who have now lived the largest part of their lives in this country, *el exilio*, the exile, meetings at private houses in Miami Beach are seen to have consequences. The actions of individuals are seen to affect events directly. Revolutions and counter-revolutions are framed in the private sector, and the state security apparatus exists exclusively to be enlisted by one or another private player. That this particular political style, indigenous to the Caribbean and to Central America, has now been naturalized in the United States is one reason why, on the flat coastal swamps of South Florida, where the palmettos once blew over the detritus of a dozen failed booms and the hotels were boarded up six months a year, there has evolved since the early New Year's morning in 1959 when Fulgencio Batista flew for the last time out of Havana (for this flight, to the Dominican Republic on an Aerovías Q DC-4, the women still wore the evening dresses in which they had gone to dinner) a settlement of considerable interest, not exactly an American city as American cities have until recently been understood but a tropical capital: long on rumor, short on memory, overbuilt on the chimera of runaway money and referring not to New York or Boston or Los Angeles or Atlanta but to Caracas and Mexico, to Havana and to Bogotá and to Paris and Madrid. Of American cities Miami has since 1959 connected only to Washington, which is the peculiarity of both places, and increasingly the warp.

In the passion of *el exilio* there are certain stations at which the converged, or colliding, fantasies of Miami and Washington appear in fixed relief. Resentments are recited, rosaries of broken promises. Occasions of error are recounted, imperfect understandings, instances in which the superimposition of Washington abstractions on Miami possibilities may or may not have been, in a word Washington came to prefer during the 1980s, flawed. On April 17, 1985, the twenty-fourth anniversary of the aborted invasion referred to by most Americans and even some Cubans as the Bay of Pigs, what seems in retrospect a particularly poignant progression of events was held in Miami to commemorate those losses suffered in 1961 at Playa Girón, on the southern coast of Matanzas Province, by the 2506 Brigade, the exile invasion force trained and supported—up to a point, the famous point, the midnight hour when John F. Kennedy sent down the decision to preserve deniability by withholding air cover—by the United States government.

The actual events of this 1985 anniversary were ritual, and as such differed only marginally from those of other years, say 1986, when Jeane Kirkpatrick would be present, to wave small souvenir flags, American and Cuban, and to speak of "how different the world would have been" had the brigade prevailed. By one minute past midnight on the morning of the 1985 anniversary, as in years before and after, some thirty members of the 2506, most of them men in their forties and fifties wearing camouflage fatigues and carrying AR-15 rifles, veterans of the invasion plus a few later recruits, had assembled at the Martyrs of Girón monument on Southwest Eighth Street in Miami and posted a color guard, to stand watch through the soft Florida night. A tape recording of "The Star Spangled Banner" had been played, and one of "La Bayamesa," the Cuban national anthem. *No temáis una muerte gloriosa*, the lyric of "La Bayamesa" runs, striking the exact note of transcendent nationalism on which the occasion turned. *Do not fear a glorious death: To die for patria is to live.*

By late morning the police had cordoned off the weathered bungalow on Southwest Ninth Street which was meant to be the Casa, Museo y Biblioteca de la Brigada 2506 del Exilio Cubano, the projected repository for such splinters of the true cross as the 2506 flag presented to John F. Kennedy at the Orange Bowl, twenty months after the Bay of Pigs, when he promised to return the flag to the brigade "in a free Havana" and took it back to Washington, later expanding its symbolic content geometrically by consigning it to storage in what explicators of this parable usually refer to as a dusty basement. On the morning of the anniversary ground was being broken for the

renovation of the bungalow, an occasion for Claude
Pepper, fresh from the continuing debate in the House
of Representatives over aid to the Nicaraguan contras,
to characterize the landing at Girón as "one of the
most heroic events in the history of the world" and
for many of those present to voice what had become
by that spring the most urgent concern of the exile
community, the very concern which now lends the
occasion its retrospective charge, that "the freedom
fighters of the eighties" not be treated by the Reagan
administration as the men of the 2506 had been treated,
or believed that they had been treated, by the Kennedy administration.

Sometimes the word used to describe that treatment was "abandonment," and sometimes the word
was "betrayal," but the meaning was the same, and
the ardor behind the words cut across all class lines,
not only that morning at the bungalow but later at
the roll call at the monument and still later, at the
Mass said that evening for the 2506 at the chapel on
Biscayne Bay which is so situated as to face Cuba.
There were men that morning in combat fatigues, but
there were also men in navy-blue blazers, with the
bright patch of the 2506 pinned discreetly to the
pocket. There were National Rifle Association wind-
breakers and there were T-shirts featuring the American flag and the legend THESE COLORS DON'T RUN and
there were crucifixes on bare skin and there were
knife sheaths on belts slung so low that Jockey shorts
showed, but there were also Brooks Brothers shirts,

and rep ties, and briefcases of supple leather. There were men who would go later that day to offices in the new glass towers along Brickell Avenue, offices with Barcelona chairs and floor-to-ceiling views of the bay and the harbor and Miami Beach and Key Biscayne, and there were men whose only offices were the gun stores and the shooting ranges and the flying clubs out off Krome Avenue, where the West Dade subdivisions give way to the Everglades and only the sudden glitter of water reveals its encroaching presence and drugs get dropped and bodies dumped.

They have been construed since as political flotsam, these men of the 2506, uniformly hard cases, drifters among the more doubtful venues serviced by Southern Air Transport, but this is misleading. Some members of the 2506 had lived in Miami since before Fidel Castro entered Havana and some had arrived as recently as 1980, the year of the Mariel exodus. Some were American citizens and some never would be, but they were all Cuban first, and they proceeded equally from a kind of collective spell, an occult enchantment, from that febrile complex of resentments and revenges and idealizations and taboos which renders exile so potent an organizing principle. They shared not just Cuba as a birthplace but Cuba as a construct, the idea of birthright lost. They shared a definition of *patria* as indivisible from personal honor, and therefore of personal honor as that which had been betrayed and must be revenged. They shared, not only with one another but with virtually every other Cuban in Miami, a political matrix in which the very shape of history, its dialectic, its tendency, had traditionally presented itself as *la lucha*, the struggle.

For most of them as children there had of course been the formative story of *la lucha* against Spain, the central scenario of nineteenth-century Cuba. For some of their fathers there had been *la lucha* against Gerardo Machado and for some of them there had been *la lucha* against Fulgencio Batista and for all of them—for those who had fought originally with the 26 Julio and for those who had fought against it, for *barbudos* and *Batistianos* alike—there was now *la lucha* on the grand canvas of a quarter century, *la lucha* purified, *la lucha* in a preservative vacuum, *la lucha* not only against Fidel Castro but against his allies, and his agents, and all those who could conceivably be believed to have aided or encouraged him.

What constituted such aid or encouragement remained the great Jesuitical subject of *el exilio*, defined and redefined, distilled finally to that point at which a notably different angle obtained on certain events in the recent American past. The 1972 burglary at the Watergate headquarters of the Democratic National Committee, say, appeared from this angle as a patriotic mission, and the Cubans who were jailed for it as *mártires de la lucha*. Mariel appeared as a betrayal on the part of yet another administration, a deal with Fidel Castro, a decision by the Carter people to preserve the status quo in Cuba by siphoning off the momentum of what could have been, in the dreamtime of *el exilio*, where the betrayal which began with the

Kennedy administration continued to the day at hand, a popular uprising. DOWN WITH THE KENNEDY-KHRU-SHCHEV PACT was the legend, in Spanish, on one of the placards bobbing for attention in front of the minicams that day. ENOUGH TREASONS. On the back of another placard there was lettered a chant: CON-TADORA / TRAIDORA / VENDA / PATRIA. That traitor who would back a political settlement in Central America, in other words, sold out his country, and so his honor.

In many ways the Bay of Pigs continued to offer Maimi an ideal narrative, one in which the men of the 2506 were forever the valiant and betrayed and the United States was forever the seducer and be-trayer and the blood of *los mártires* remained forever fresh. When the names of the 114 brigade members who died in Cuba were read off that day at the Playa Girón monument, the survivors had called out the responses in unison, the rhythm building, clenched fists thrust toward the sky: *Presente*, 114 times. The women, in silk dresses and high-heeled sandals, dabbed at their eyes behind dark glasses. "*Es triste*," one woman murmured, again and again, to no one in par-ticular.

La tristeza de Miami. "We must attempt to strengthen the non-Batista democratic anti-Castro forces in exile," a Kennedy campaign statement had declared in 1960, and Miami had for a time believed John F. Kennedy a communicant in its faith. "We cannot have the United States walk away from one of the greatest moral challenges in postwar history," Ronald Reagan had declared two nights before this

1985 anniversary of the Bay of Pigs, at a Nicaraguan Refugee Fund benefit dinner in Washington, and Miami once again believed an American president a communicant in its faith. Even the paper thimbles of sweet Cuban coffee distributed after the 2506 Mass that April evening in Miami, on the steps of the chapel which faces Cuba and has over its altar a sequined Virgin, a Virgin dressed for her *quince*, had the aspect of a secular communion, the body and blood of *patria*, *machismo*, *la lucha*, sentimental trinity. That *la lucha* had become, during the years since the Bay of Pigs, a matter of assassinations and bombings on the streets of American cities, of plots and counterplots and covert dealings involving American citizens and American institutions, of attitudes and actions which had shadowed the abrupt termination of two American presidencies and would eventually shadow the immobilization of a third, was a peculiarity left, that one evening, officially unexplored.

TWO

2

"THE general wildness, the eternal labyrinths of waters and marshes, interlocked and apparently never ending; the whole surrounded by interminable swamps. . . . Here I am then in the Floridas, thought I," John James Audubon wrote to the editor of *The Monthly American Journal of Geology and Natural Science* during the course of an 1831 foray in the territory then still called the Floridas. The place came first, and to touch down there is to begin to understand why at least six administrations now have found South Florida so fecund a colony. I never passed through security for a flight to Miami without experiencing a certain weightlessness, the heightened wariness of having left the developed world for a more fluid atmosphere, one in which the native distrust of extreme possibilities that tended to ground the temperate United States in an obeisance to democratic institutions seemed rooted, if at all, only shallowly. At the gate for such flights the preferred language was already Spanish. Delays were explained by weather in Panama. The very names of the scheduled destinations suggested a world in which many evangelical inclinations had historically been accommodated, many yearnings toward empire indulged.

The Eastern 5:59 P.M. from New York/Kennedy to Miami and Panama and Santiago and Buenos Aires carried in its magazine racks, along with the usual pristine copies of *Golf* and *Ebony* and *U.S. News & World Report*, a monthly called *South: The Third World Magazine*, edited in London and tending to brisk backgrounders on coup rumors and capital flight.

In Miami itself this kind of news was considerably less peripheral than it might have seemed farther north, since to set foot in South Florida was already to be in a place where coup rumors and capital flight were precisely what put money on the street, and also what took it off. The charts on the wall in a Coral Gables investment office gave the time in Panama, San Salvador, Asunción. A chain of local gun shops advertised, as a "Father's Day Sale," the semiautomatic Intratec TEC-9, with extra ammo clip, case, and flash suppressor, reduced from $347.80 to $249.95 and available on layaway. I recall picking up the *Miami Herald* one morning in July of 1985 to read that the Howard Johnson's hotel near the Miami airport had been offering "guerrilla discounts," rooms at seventeen dollars a day under what an employee, when pressed by the *Herald* reporter, described as "a freedom fighters program" that was "supposed to be under wraps."

As in other parts of the world where the citizens shop for guerrilla discounts and bargains in semiautomatic weapons, there was in Miami an advanced interest in personal security. The security installations in certain residential neighborhoods could have been transplanted intact from Bogotá or San Salvador, and even modest householders had detailed information about perimeter defenses, areas of containment, motion monitors and closed-circuit television surveillance. Decorative grilles on doors and windows turned out to have a defensive intent. Break-ins were referred to by the Metro-Dade Police Department as "home invasions," a locution which tended to suggest a city under systematic siege. A firm specializing in security for the home and automobile offered to install bulletproof windows tested to withstand a 7.62mm NATO round of ammunition, for example one fired by an M60. A ten-page pamphlet found, along with $119,-500 in small bills, in the Turnberry Isle apartment of an accused cocaine importer gave these tips for maintaining a secure profile: "Try to imitate an American in all his habits. Mow the lawn, wash the car, etc. . . . Have an occasional barbecue, inviting trusted relatives." The wary citizen could on other occasions, the pamphlet advised, "appear as the butler of the house. To any question, he can answer: the owners are traveling."

This assumption of extralegal needs dominated the advertisements for more expensive residential properties. The Previews brochure for a house on Star Island, built originally as the Miami Beach Yacht Club and converted to residential use in the 1920s by Hetty Green's son, emphasized, in the headline, not the house's twenty-one rooms, not its multiple pools, not even its 255 feet of bay frontage, but its "Unusual Security and Ready Access to the Ocean." Grove

Isle, a luxury condominium complex with pieces by Isamu Noguchi and Alexander Calder and Louise Nevelson in its sculpture garden, presented itself as "a bridge away from Coconut Grove," which meant, in the local code, that access was controlled, in this case by one of the "double security" systems favored in new Miami buildings, requiring that the permit acquired at the gate, or "perimeter," be surrendered at the second line of defense, the entrance to the building itself. A bridge, I was told by several people in Miami, was a good thing to have between oneself and the city, because it could be drawn up, or blocked, during times of unrest.

For a city even then being presented, in news reports and in magazine pieces and even in advertising and fashion promotions which had adopted their style from the television show "Miami Vice," as a rich and wicked pastel boomtown, Miami seemed, at the time I began spending time there, rather spectacularly depressed, again on the southern model. There were new condominiums largely unsold. There were new office towers largely unleased. There were certain signs of cutting and running among those investors who had misread the constant cash moving in and out of Miami as the kind of reliable American money they understood, and been left holding the notes. Helmsley-Spear, it was reported, had let an undeveloped piece on Biscayne Bay go into foreclosure, saving itself $3 million a year in taxes. Tishman Speyer had jettisoned plans for an $800-million medical complex in Broward

County. WELL-HEELED INVESTORS RETURNING NORTH
was a *Herald* headline in June of 1985. COSTLY CONDOS
THREATENED WITH MASSIVE FORECLOSURES was a *Herald* headline in August of 1985. FORECLOSURES SOARING
IN S. FLORIDA was a *Herald* headline in March of 1986.

The feel was that of a Latin capital, a year or two
away from a new government. Space in shopping
malls was unrented, or rented to the wrong tenants.
There were too many shoe stores for an American
city, and video arcades. There were also too many
public works projects: a new mass transit system
which did not effectively transport anyone, a projected
"people mover" around the downtown area which
would, it was said, salvage the new mass transit system. On my first visits to Miami the gleaming new
Metrorail cars glided empty down to the Dadeland
Mall and back, ghost trains above the jammed traffic
on the South Dixie Highway. When I returned a few
months later service had already been cut back, and
the billion-dollar Metrorail ran only until early evening.

A tropical entropy seemed to prevail, defeating
grand schemes even as they were realized. Minor drug
deals took place beneath the then unfinished people-
mover tracks off Biscayne Boulevard, and plans were
under way for yet another salvage operation, "Biscayne Centrum," a twenty-eight-acre sports arena and
convention hall that could theoretically be reached by
either Metrorail or people mover and offered the further advantage, since its projected site lay within the
area sealed off during the 1982 Overtown riot, a dis-

trict of generally apathetic but occasionally volatile poverty, of defoliating at least twenty-eight acres of potential trouble. ARENA FINANCING PLAN RELIES ON HOTEL GUESTS was a *Herald* headline one morning. S. FLORIDA HOTEL ROOMS GET EMPTIER was a *Herald* headline four months later. A business reporter for the *Herald* asked a local real-estate analyst when he thought South Florida would turn around. "Tell me when South America is going to turn around," the analyst said.

Meanwhile the construction cranes still hovered on the famous new skyline, which, floating as it did between a mangrove swamp and a barrier reef, had a kind of perilous attraction, like a mirage. I recall walking one October evening through the marble lobby of what was then the Pavillon Hotel, part of the massive new Miami Center which Pietro Belluschi had designed for a Virginia developer named Theodore Gould. There was in this vast travertine public space that evening one other person, a young Cuban woman in a short black dinner dress who seemed to be in charge of table arrangements for a gala not in evidence. I could hear my heels clicking on the marble. I could hear the young woman in the black taffeta dinner dress drumming her lacquered fingernails on the table at which she sat. It occurred to me that she and I might be the only people in the great empty skyline itself. Later that week control of the Pavillon, and of Miami Center, passed, the latest chapter in a short dolorous history of hearings and defaults and Chapter 11 filings, from Theodore Gould to the Bank of New York, and it was announced that the Inter-Continental chain would henceforth operate the hotel. The occupancy rate at the Pavillon was, at the time Inter-Continental assumed its management, 7 percent. Theodore Gould was said by the chairman of the Greater Miami Chamber of Commerce to have made "a very unique contribution to downtown Miami."

3

DURING the spring when I began visiting Miami all of Florida was reported to be in drought, with dropping water tables and unfilled aquifers and SAVE WATER signs, but drought, in a part of the world which would be in its natural state a shelf of porous oolitic limestone covered most of the year by a shallow sheet flow of fresh water, proved relative. During this drought the city of Coral Gables continued, as it had every night since 1924, to empty and refill its Venetian Pool with fresh unchlorinated water, 820,000 gallons a day out of the water supply and into the storm sewer. There was less water than there might have been in the Biscayne Aquifer but there was water everywhere above it. There were rains so hard that windshield wipers stopped working and cars got swamped and stalled on I-95. There was water roiling and bubbling over the underwater lights in decorative pools. There was water sluicing off the six-story canted window at the Omni, a hotel from which it was possible to see, in the Third World way, both the slums of Overtown and those island houses with the Unusual Security and Ready Access to the Ocean, equally wet. Water plashed off banana palms, water puddled on flat roofs, water streamed down the CARNE

U.S. GOOD & U.S. STANDARD signs on Flagler Street.
Water rocked the impounded drug boats which lined
the Miami River and water lapped against the causeways on the bay. I got used to the smell of incipient
mildew in my clothes. I stuffed Kleenex in wet shoes
and stopped expecting them to dry.

A certain liquidity suffused everything about the
place. Causeways and bridges and even Brickell Avenue did not stay put but rose and fell, allowing the
masts of ships to glide among the marble and glass
facades of the unleased office buildings. The buildings
themselves seemed to swim free against the sky: there
had grown up in Miami during the recent money
years an architecture which appeared to have slipped
its moorings, a not inappropriate style for a terrain
with only a provisional claim on being land at all. Surfaces were reflective, opalescent. Angles were oblique,
intersecting to disorienting effect. The Arquitectonica
office, which produced the celebrated glass condominium on Brickell Avenue with the fifty-foot cube
cut from its center, the frequently photographed "sky
patio" in which there floated a palm tree, a Jacuzzi,
and a lipstick-red spiral staircase, accompanied its ele-
vations with crayon sketches, all moons and starry
skies and airborne maidens, as in a Chagall. Skidmore,
Owings and Merrill managed, in its Southeast Finan-
cial Center, the considerable feat of rendering fifty-
five stories of polished gray granite incorporeal, a sky-
blue illusion.

Nothing about Miami was exactly fixed, or hard.
Hard consonants were missing from the local speech

patterns, in English as well as in Spanish. Local money tended to move on hydraulic verbs: when it was not being washed it was being diverted, or channeled through Mexico, or turned off in Washington. Local stories tended to turn on underwater plot points, submerged snappers: on unsoundable extradition proceedings in the Bahamas, say, or fluid connections with the Banco Nacional de Colombia. I recall trying to touch the bottom of one such story in the *Herald*, about six hand grenades which had just been dug up in the bay-front backyard of a Biscayne Boulevard pawnbroker who had been killed in his own bed a few years before, shot at close range with a .25-caliber automatic pistol.

There were some other details on the surface of this story, for example the wife who fired the .25-caliber automatic pistol and the nineteen-year-old daughter who was up on federal weapons charges and the flight attendant who rented the garage apartment and said that the pawnbroker had collected "just basic things like rockets, just defused things," but the underwater narrative included, at last sounding, the Central Intelligence Agency (with which the pawnbroker was said to have been associated), the British intelligence agency MI6 (with which the pawnbroker was also said to have been associated), the late Anastasio Somoza Debayle (whose family the pawnbroker was said to have spirited into Miami shortly before the regime fell in Managua), the late shah of Iran (whose presence in Panama was said to have queered an arms deal about which the pawnbroker had been told),

Dr. Josef Mengele (for whom the pawnbroker was said to be searching), and a Pompano Beach resident last seen cruising Miami in a cinnamon-colored Cadillac Sedan de Ville and looking to buy, he said for the Salvadoran insurgents, a million rounds of ammunition, thirteen thousand assault rifles, and "at least a couple" of jeep-mounted machine guns.

In this mood Miami seemed not a city at all but a tale, a romance of the tropics, a kind of waking dream in which any possibility could and would be accommodated. The most ordinary morning, say at the courthouse, could open onto the distinctly lurid. "I don't think he came out with me, that's all," I recall hearing someone say one day in an elevator at the Miami federal courthouse. His voice had kept rising. "What happened to all that stuff about how next time, he gets twenty keys, he could run wherever-it-is-Idaho, now he says he wouldn't know what to do with five keys, what is this shit?" His companion had shrugged. We had continued in silence to the main floor. Outside one courtroom that day a group of Colombians, the women in silk shirts and Chanel necklaces and Charles Jourdan suede pumps, the children in appliquéd dresses from Baby Dior, had been waiting for the decision in a pretrial detention hearing, one in which the government was contending that the two defendants, who between them lived in houses in which eighty-three kilos of cocaine and a million-three in cash had been found, failed to qualify as good bail risks.

"That doesn't make him a longtime drug dealer," one of the two defense lawyers, both of whom were Anglo and one of whom drove a Mercedes 380 SEL with the license plate DEFENSE, had argued about the million-three in cash. "That could be one transaction." Across the hall that day closing arguments were being heard in a boat case, a "boat case" being one in which a merchant or fishing vessel has been boarded and drugs seized and eight or ten Colombian crew members arrested, the kind of case in which pleas were typically entered so that one of the Colombians would get eighteen months and the others deported. There were never any women in Chanel necklaces around a boat case, and the lawyers (who were usually hired and paid for not by the defendants but by the unnamed owner of the "load," or shipment) tended to be Cuban. "You had the great argument, you got to give me some good ideas," one of the eight Cuban defense lawyers on this case joked with the prosecutor during a recess. "But you haven't heard my argument yet," another of the defense lawyers said. "The stuff about communism. Fabulous closing argument."

Just as any morning could turn lurid, any moment could turn final, again as in a dream. "I heard a loud, short noise and then there was just a plain moment of dullness," the witness to a shooting in a Miami Beach supermarket parking lot told the *Herald*. "There was no one around except me and two bagboys." I happened to be in the coroner's office one morning when autopsies were being performed on the bodies of two Mariels, shot and apparently pushed from a car on

I-95 about nine the evening before, another plain moment of dullness. The story had been on television an hour or two after it happened: I had seen the crime site on the eleven o'clock news, and had not expected to see the victims in the morning. "When he came here in Mariel he stayed at our house but he didn't get along with my mom," a young girl was saying in the anteroom to one of the detectives working the case. "These two guys were killed together," the detective had pressed. "They probably knew each other."

"For sure," the young girl had said, agreeably. Inside the autopsy room the hands of the two young men were encased in the brown paper bags which indicated that the police had not yet taken what they needed for laboratory studies. Their flesh had the marbleized yellow look of the recently dead. There were other bodies in the room, in various stages of autopsy, and a young woman in a white coat taking eyes, for the eye bank. "Who are we going to start on next?" one of the assistant medical examiners was saying. "The fat guy? Let's do the fat guy."

It was even possible to enter the waking dream without leaving the house, just by reading the *Herald*. A Mariel named Jose "Coca-Cola" Yero gets arrested, with nine acquaintances, in a case involving 1,664 pounds of cocaine, a thirty-seven-foot Cigarette boat named *The Connection*, two Lamborghinis, a million-six in cash, a Mercedes 500 SEL with another $350,000 in cash in the trunk, one dozen Rolex watches color-coordinated to match Jose "Coca-Cola" Yero's wardrobe, and various houses in Dade and Palm Beach counties, a search of one of which turns up not just a photograph of Jose "Coca-Cola" Yero face down in a pile of white powder but also a framed poster of Al Pacino as Tony Montana, the Mariel who appears at a dramatic moment in *Scarface* face down in a pile of white powder. "They got swept up in the fast lane," a Metro-Dade narcotics detective advises the *Herald*. "The fast lane is what put this whole group in jail." A young woman in South Palm Beach goes out to the parking lot of her parents' condominium and gets into her 1979 Pontiac Firebird, opens the T-top, starts the ignition and loses four toes when the bomb goes off. "She definitely knows someone is trying to kill her," the sheriff's investigator tells the *Herald*. "She knew they were coming, but she didn't know when."

Surfaces tended to dissolve here. Clear days ended less so. I recall an October Sunday when my husband and I were taken, by Gene Miller, a *Herald* editor who had won two Pulitzer Prizes for investigative reporting and who had access to season tickets exactly on the fifty-yard line at the Orange Bowl, to see the Miami Dolphins beat the Pittsburgh Steelers, 21–17. In the row below us the former Dolphin quarterback Earl Morrall signed autographs for the children who wriggled over seats to slip him their programs and steal surreptitious glances at his Super Bowl ring. A few rows back an Anglo teenager in sandals and shorts and a black T-shirt smoked a marijuana cigarette in full view of the Hispanic police officer behind him. Hot dogs were passed, and Coca-Cola spilled. Sony

Watchmans were compared, for the definition on the instant replay. The NBC cameras dollied along the sidelines and the Dolphin cheerleaders kneeled on their white pom-poms and there was a good deal of talk about red dogging and weak secondaries and who would be seen and what would be eaten in New Orleans, come Super Bowl weekend.

The Miami on display in the Orange Bowl that Sunday afternoon would have seemed another Miami altogether, one with less weather and harder, more American surfaces, but by dinner we were slipping back into the tropical: in a virtually empty restaurant on top of a virtually empty condominum off Biscayne Boulevard, with six people at the table, one of whom was Gene Miller and one of whom was Martin Dardis, who as the chief investigator for the state attorney's office in Miami had led Carl Bernstein through the local angles on Watergate and who remained a walking data bank on CDs at the Biscayne Bank and on who called who on what payoff and on how to follow a money chain, we sat and we talked and we watched a storm break over Biscayne Bay. Sheets of warm rain washed down the big windows. Lightning began to fork somewhere around Bal Harbour. Gene Miller mentioned the Alberto Duque trial, then entering its fourth week at the federal courthouse, the biggest bank fraud case ever tried in the United States. Martin Dardis mentioned the ESM Government Securities collapse, just then breaking into a fraud case maybe bigger than the Duque.

The lightning was no longer forking now but illuminating the entire sky, flashing a dead strobe white, turning the bay fluorescent and the islands black, as if in negative. I sat and I listened to Gene Miller and Martin Dardis discuss these old and new turns in the underwater narrative and I watched the lightning backlight the islands. During the time I had spent in Miami many people had mentioned, always as something extraordinary, something I should have seen if I wanted to understand Miami, the *Surrounded Islands* project executed in Biscayne Bay in 1983 by the Bulgarian artist Christo. *Surrounded Islands*, which had involved surrounding eleven islands with two-hundred-foot petals, or skirts, of pink polypropylene fabric, had been mentioned both by people who were knowledgeable about conceptual art and by people who had not before heard and could not then recall the name of the man who had surrounded the islands. All had agreed. It seemed that the pink had shimmered in the water. It seemed that the pink had kept changing color, fading and reemerging with the movement of the water and the clouds and the sun and the night lights. It seemed that this period when the pink was in the water had for many people exactly defined, as the backlit islands and the fluorescent water and the voices at the table were that night defining for me, Miami.

4

On my first visits to Miami I was always being told that there were places I should not go. There were things I should and should not do. I should not walk the block and a half from the Omni to the *Herald* alone after dark. I should lock my car doors when I drove at night. If I hit a red light as I was about to enter I-95 I should not stop but look both ways, and accelerate. I should not drive through Liberty City, or walk around Overtown. If I had occasion to drive through what was called "the black Grove," those several dozen blocks of project housing which separated the expensive greenery of Coral Gables from the expensive greenery of Coconut Grove, I should rethink my route, avoid at all costs the territory of the disentitled, which in fact was hard to do, since Miami was a city, like so many to the south of it, in which it was possible to pass from walled enclaves to utter desolation while changing stations on the car radio.

In the end I went without incident to all of the places I had been told not to go, and did not or did do most of the things I had been told to do or not to do, but the subtext of what I had been told, that this was a city in which black people and white people viewed each other with some discontent, stayed with me, if only because the most dramatic recent season of that discontent, the spring of 1980, the season when certain disruptive events in Havana happened to coincide with a drama then being played out in a Florida courtroom, still figured so large in the local memory. Many people in Miami mentioned the spring of 1980 to me, speaking always of its "mood," which appeared to have been one of collective fever. In the spring of 1980 everyone had been, it was said, "nervous," or "tense." This tension had built, it was said, "to a point of just no return," or "to the breaking point." "It could drive you mad, just waiting for something to happen," one woman said. "The Cuban kids were all out leaning on their horns and the blacks were all out sitting on their porches," someone else said. "You knew it was going to happen but you didn't know when. And anyway it was going to happen. There was no doubt about that. It was like, well, a bad dream. When you try to wake up and you can't."

The Miami part of what happened that spring, the part people in Miami refer to as "McDuffie," had its proximate beginning early on the morning of December 17, 1979, when a thirty-three-year-old black insurance agent named Arthur McDuffie was said by police to have made a rolling stop at a red light, to have executed the maneuver called "popping a wheelie" on his borrowed Kawasaki motorcycle, and to have given the finger to a Dade County Public Safety Department officer parked nearby. The officer gave chase. By the time Arthur McDuffie was apprehended, eight minutes later, more than a dozen Dade County and city of Miami police units had converged on the scene.

Accounts of the next several minutes conflict. What is known is that at some point a rescue unit was called, for the victim of an "accident," and that four days later Arthur McDuffie died, without regaining consciousness, in Jackson Memorial Hospital. On March 31, 1980, four Dade County Public Safety Department officers, all four of them white, each charged with having played some role in the beating of Arthur McDuffie or in the subsequent attempt to make his injuries seem the result of a motorcycle accident, went on trial before an all-white jury in Tampa, where the case had been moved after a Miami judge granted a change of venue with these words: "This case is a time bomb. I don't want to see it go off in my courtroom or in this community."

The Havana part of what happened in the spring of 1980 was also a time bomb. There had been all that spring a dispute between Fidel Castro and the government of Peru over the disposition of a handful of disaffected Cubans who had claimed asylum at the Peruvian embassy in Havana. Castro wanted the Cubans turned out. Peru insisted that they be brought to Lima. It was April 4, four days after jury selection began in the McDuffie case in Tampa, when the Cuban government, as an apparently quixotic move in this dispute, bulldozed down the gates at the Peruvian embassy in Havana and set into motion, whether deliberately or inadvertently, that chain of events referred to as

"Mariel," by which people in Miami mean not just the place and not just the boatlift and not just what many see as the "trick," the way in which Fidel Castro managed to take his own problem and make it Miami's, but the entire range of dislocations attendant upon the unloading of 125,000 refugees, 26,000 of them with prison records, onto an already volatile community.

The first Mariel refugees arrived in South Florida on April 21, 1980. By May 17, the day the McDuffie case went to the jury in Tampa, there were already some 57,000 Mariels camped under the bleachers at the Orange Bowl and in makeshift tent cities in the Orange Bowl parking area and on the public land under I-95, downtown, in the most visible and frequently traveled part of the city, in case it had escaped anybody's notice that the needs of the black community might not in the immediate future have Miami's full attention. May 17 was a Saturday. The temperature was in the mid-seventies. There was, in Miami, no rain in view.

There appears to have been an astonishing innocence about what happened that day. In another part of the country the judge in a trial as sensitive as the McDuffie trial might not have allowed the case to go to the jury on a clear Saturday morning, but the judge in Tampa did. In another part of the country the jury in such a case might not have brought in its verdicts, complete acquittal for all four defendants, in just two hours and forty-five minutes, which came down to something less than forty-two minutes per defendant, but the jury in Tampa did, in many ways predictably, for among the citizens of South Florida the urge to conciliate one another remained remarkably undeveloped. The president of the Orange Bowl Committee, which pretty much represents the established order in Miami, thought as recently as 1985, and said so, for attribution, that it was "not offensive" for the committee to entertain the participating college teams at the Indian Creek Country Club, which admitted no blacks or Jews as members but did allow them to visit the club as guests at private parties. "At the hospital where I work, the black doctors are intellectually fine and wonderful people, but they aren't able to handle the cosmopolitan aspects of circulating in society," a Miami surgeon said a few weeks later, also for attribution, to the *Herald* reporter who had asked him about restrictive policies at another local institution, the Bath Club, on Collins Avenue in Miami Beach.

Symbolic moves seemed to be missing here. A University of Miami study released the month of the 1968 Miami Riot had found it necessary to suggest that local black males resented being addressed by police as "boy," or "nigger." When a delegation of black citizens had asked the same year that a certain police officer be transferred, after conduct which had troubled the community, off his Liberty City beat, they were advised by the Miami chief of police that their complaint was "silly." Several weeks later it was reported that the officer in question and his partner had picked up a black seventeen-year-old, charged him with carrying a concealed knife, forced him to strip naked, and dangled him by his heels a hundred feet over the Miami River, from an unfinished span of the Dolphin Expressway.

During the twelve years between the 1968 Miami Riot and the Saturday in 1980 when the McDuffie case went to the jury, there had been, in Dade County, thirteen occasions on which the rage of some part of the black community went, for periods of time ranging from a few hours to a few days, out of control. This regular evidence of discontent notwithstanding, those gestures with which other troubled cities gradually learn to accommodate their citizens seemed not, in South Florida, to take hold. Blacks continued to be excluded for cause from juries in trials involving police officers accused of killing blacks. The juries in such cases continued to stay out two hours, and to bring in acquittals, on clear days, in the summer.

The McDuffie acquittals were on the Associated Press wire, that clear Saturday in 1980, by 2:42 P.M. The first police call reporting rioting in Liberty City came in at 6:02 P.M., from Miami Police Department Unit 621. By 9:44 P.M., when a call was placed to Tallahassee asking that the National Guard be sent in, there was rioting not only in Liberty City but in Overtown and in the black Grove and around the entire Metro Justice complex, where doctors and nurses answering emergency calls to Jackson Memorial Hospital were being stoned and beaten and the Metro Justice building itself was being torched. Four days later, when the 1980 Liberty City Riot, called that because

Liberty City was where it had begun, had run its course, there were eighteen dead or fatally injured, eight of them whites who had driven down the wrong streets and been stoned or doused with gasoline and set afire or, in the case of one, a twenty-two-year-old Burdines warehouse loader on his way home from a day at the beach with his girlfriend and younger brother, dragged from the car to be beaten, kicked, struck not only with bottles and bricks and a twenty-three-pound chunk of concrete but also with a *Miami Herald* street dispenser, shot, stabbed with a screwdriver, run over by a green Cadillac and left, one ear cut off and lying on his chest and his tongue cut out, with a red rose in his mouth.

An instinct for self-preservation would have seemed at this point to encourage negotiations, or at least the appearance of negotiations, but few lessons get learned in tropical cities under attack from their own citizens. Lines only harden. Positions become more fixed, and privileges more fiercely defended. In December of 1982 another police killing of another black man occasioned another riot, the 1982 Overtown Riot, on the second night of which there happened to be held, in the ballroom of the Surf Club on Collins Avenue, which numbered among its 680 members no blacks and no Jews, one of the most expensive parties given that year in Miami, a debutante party at which actors performed the story of Little Red Riding Hood under two hundred freshly cut fir trees arranged to represent the Black Forest of Bavaria. In this case too the police officer in question, a Cuban, was eventually tried before an all-white jury, which again stayed out two hours and again brought in an acquittal. This verdict came in early one Thursday evening in March of 1984, and order was restored in Miami just after midnight on Saturday morning, which was applauded locally as progress, not even a riot.

There are between the street and the lobby levels of the Omni International Hotel on Biscayne Boulevard, one block east of the hundred-block area sealed off by police during the 1982 Overtown Riot, two levels of shops and movie theaters and carnival attractions: a mall, so designed that the teenagers, most of them black and most of them male, who hang out around the carousel in the evenings, waiting for a movie to break or for a turn at the Space Walk or at the Sea of Balls or just for something to happen, can look up to the Omni ballroom and lobby levels, but only with some ingenuity reach them, since a steel grille blocks the floating stairway after dark and armed security men patrol the elevator areas. The visible presence of this more or less forbidden upstairs lends the mall in the evening an unspecific atmosphere of incipient trouble, an uneasiness which has its equivalent in the hotel itself, where the insistent and rather sinister music from the carousel downstairs comes to suggest, particularly on those weekend nights when the mall is at its loosest and the hotel often given over to one or another of the lavish *quinces* or charity galas which fill the local Cuban calendar, a violent night world just underfoot, and perhaps not underfoot for long.

Not often does a social dynamic seem to present itself in a single tableau, but at the Omni in Miami one did, and during the time I spent there I came to see the hotel and its mall as the most theatrical possible illustration of how a native proletariat can be left behind in a city open to the convulsions of the Third World, something which had happened in the United States first and most dramatically in Miami but had been happening since in other parts of the country. Black Miami had of course been particularly unprepared to have the world move in. Its common experience was of the cracker South. Black assertiveness had been virtually nonexistent, black political organization absent. Into the 1960s, according to *The Miami Riot of 1980*, a study of the Liberty City Riot by Bruce Porter of Brooklyn College and Marvin Dunn of Florida International University, the latter a black candidate for mayor of Miami who lost in 1985 to a Cuban, Xavier Suarez, Miami blacks did not swim at Dade County beaches. When Miami blacks paid taxes at the Dade County Courthouse they did so at a separate window, and when Miami blacks shopped at Burdines, where they were allowed to buy although not to try on clothes, they did so without using the elevators.

This had been a familiar enough pattern throughout the South, but something else had happened here. Desegregation had not just come hard and late to South Florida but it had also coincided, as it had not in other parts of the South, with another disruption of the local status quo, the major Cuban influx, which meant that jobs and services which might have helped awaken an inchoate black community went instead to Cubans, who tended to be overtrained but willing. Havana bankers took jobs as inventory clerks at forty-five dollars a week. Havana newspaper publishers drove taxis. That these were the men in black tie who now danced with the women in the Chanel and Valentino evening dresses on the ballroom level of the Omni was an irony lost in its precise detail, although not in its broad outline, on the sons of the men who did not get jobs as inventory clerks or taxi drivers, the children downstairs, in the high-topped sneakers, fanning in packs through the dim avenues of the locked-up mall.

5

Oɴ the one hundred and fiftieth anniversary of the founding of Dade County, in February of 1986, the *Miami Herald* asked four prominent amateurs of local history to name "the ten people and the ten events that had the most impact on the county's history." Each of the four submitted his or her own list of "The Most Influential People in Dade's History," and among the names mentioned were Julia Tuttle ("pioneer businesswoman"), Henry Flagler ("brought the Florida East Coast Railway to Miami"), Alexander Orr, Jr. ("started the research that saved Miami's drinking water from salt"), Everest George Sewell ("publicized the city and fostered its deepwater seaport"), Carl Fisher ("creator of Miami Beach"), Hugh M. Anderson ("to whom we owe Biscayne Boulevard, Miami Shores, and more"), Charles H. Crandon ("father of Dade County's park system"), Glenn Curtiss ("developer and promoter of the area's aviation potential"), and James L. Knight ("whose creative management enabled the *Miami Herald* to become a force for good"), this last nominee the choice of a retired *Herald* editorial writer.

There were more names. There were John Pennekamp ("conceived Dade's metropolitan form of gov-

ernment and fathered the Everglades National Park")
and Father Theodore Gibson ("inspirational spokesman for racial justice and social change"). There were
Maurice Ferre ("mayor for twelve years") and Mar-
jorie Stoneman Douglas ("indefatigable environmen-
talist") and Dr. Bowman F. Ashe ("first and longtime
president of the University of Miami"). There was
David Fairchild, who "popularized tropical plants and
horticulture that have made the county a more attractive place to live." There was William A. Graham,
"whose Miami Lakes is a model for real estate devel-
opment," Miami Lakes being the area developed by
William A. Graham and his brother, Senator Bob
Graham, at the time of Dade's one hundred and fiftieth anniversary the governor of Florida, on three
thousand acres their father had just west of the Opa-
Locka Airport.

There was another Graham, Ernest R., the father
of Bob and William A., nominated for his "experi-
ments with sugarcane culture and dairying." There
was another developer, John Collins, as in Collins Avenue, Miami Beach. There were, as a dual entry, Richard Fitzpatrick, who "owned four square miles between what is now Northeast 14th Street and Coconut
Grove," and William F. English, who "platted the village of Miami." There was Dr. James M. Jackson, an
early Miami physician. There was Napoleon Bonaparte
Broward, the governor of Florida who initiated the
draining of the Everglades. There appeared on three
of the four lists the name of the developer of Coral
Gables, George Merrick. There appeared on one of

the four lists the name of the coach of the Miami Dolphins, Don Shula.

On none of these lists of "The Most Influential People in Dade's History" did the name Fidel Castro appear, nor for that matter did the name of any Cuban, although the presence of Cubans in Dade County did not go entirely unnoted by the *Herald* panel. When it came to naming the Ten Most Important "Events," as opposed to "People," all four panelists mentioned the arrival of the Cubans, but at slightly off angles ("Mariel Boatlift of 1980" was the way one panelist saw it), and as if this arrival had been just another of those isolated disasters or innovations which deflect the course of any growing community, on an approximate par with the other events mentioned, for example the Freeze of 1895, the Hurricane of 1926, the opening of the Dixie Highway, the establishment of Miami International Airport, and the adoption, in 1957, of the metropolitan form of government, "enabling the Dade County Commission to provide urban services to the increasingly populous unincorporated area."

This set of mind, in which the local Cuban community was seen as a civic challenge determinedly met, was not uncommon among Anglos to whom I talked in Miami, many of whom persisted in the related illusions that the city was small, manageable, prosperous in a predictable broad-based way, southern in a progressive sunbelt way, American, and belonged to them. In fact 43 percent of the population of Dade County was by that time "Hispanic," which meant mostly Cuban. Fifty-six percent of the population of Miami itself was Hispanic. The most visible new buildings on the Miami skyline, the Arquitectonica buildings along Brickell Avenue, were by a firm with a Cuban founder. There were Cubans in the board rooms of the major banks, Cubans in the clubs that did not admit Jews or blacks, and four Cubans in the most recent mayoralty campaign, two of whom, Raul Masvidal and Xavier Suarez, had beaten out the incumbent and all other candidates to meet in a runoff, and one of whom, Xavier Suarez, a thirty-six-year-old lawyer who had been brought from Cuba to the United States as a child, was by then mayor of Miami.

The entire tone of the city, the way people looked and talked and met one another, was Cuban. The very image the city had begun presenting of itself, what was then its newfound glamour, its "hotness" (hot colors, hot vice, shady dealings under the palm trees), was that of prerevolutionary Havana, as perceived by Americans. There was even in the way women dressed in Miami a definable Havana look, a more distinct emphasis on the hips and décolletage, more black, more veiling, a generalized flirtatiousness of style not then current in American cities. In the shoe departments at Burdines and Jordan Marsh there were more platform soles than there might have been in another American city, and fewer displays of the running-shoe ethic. I recall being struck, during an afternoon spent at La Liga Contra el Cancer, a prominent exile charity which raises money to help cancer patients, by the appearance of the volunteers who had met that day to stuff envelopes for a benefit. Their hair was sleek, of a slightly other period, immaculate page boys and French twists. They wore Bruno Magli pumps, and silk and linen dresses of considerable expense. There seemed to be a preference for strictest gray or black, but the effect remained lush, tropical, like a room full of perfectly groomed mangoes.

This was not, in other words, an invisible 56 percent of the population. Even the social notes in *Diario Las Americas* and in *El Herald*, the daily Spanish edition of the *Herald* written and edited for *el exilio*, suggested a dominant culture, one with money to spend and a notable willingness to spend it in public. La Liga Contra el Cancer alone sponsored, in a single year, two benefit dinner dances, one benefit ball, a benefit children's fashion show, a benefit telethon, a benefit exhibition of jewelry, a benefit presentation of Miss Universe contestants, and a benefit showing, with Saks Fifth Avenue and chicken *vol-au-vent*, of the Adolfo (as it happened, a Cuban) fall collection. One morning *El Herald* would bring news of the gala at the Pavillon of the Amigos Latinamericanos del Museo de Ciencia y Planetarium; another morning, of an upcoming event at the Big Five Club, a Miami club founded by former members of five fashionable clubs in prerevolutionary Havana: a *coctel*, or cocktail party, at which tables would be assigned for yet another gala, the annual "Baile Imperial de las Rosas" of the American Cancer Society, Hispanic Ladies Auxiliary. Some members of the community were honoring Miss America Latina with dinner dancing at the Doral. Some were being honored themselves, at the Spirit of Excel-

lence Awards Dinner at the Omni. Some were said to
be enjoying the skiing at Vail; others to prefer Barilo-
che, in Argentina. Some were reported unable to attend (but sending checks for) the gala at the Pavillon
of the Amigos Latinamericanos del Museo de Ciencia
y Planetarium because of a scheduling conflict, with
el coctel de Paula Hawkins.

Fete followed fete, all high visibility. Almost any
day it was possible to drive past the limestone arches
and fountains which marked the boundaries of Coral
Gables and see little girls being photographed in the
tiaras and ruffled hoop skirts and maribou-trimmed illusion capes they would wear at their *quinces*, the
elaborate fifteenth-birthday parties at which the community's female children came of official age. The favored facial expression for a *quince* photograph was a
classic smolder. The favored backdrop was one suggesting Castilian grandeur, which was how the Coral
Gables arches happened to figure. Since the idealization of the virgin implicit in the *quince* could exist
only in the presence of its natural foil, *machismo*,
there was often a brother around, or a boyfriend.
There was also a mother, in dark glasses, not only to
protect the symbolic virgin but to point out the better
angle, the more aristocratic location. The *quinceañera*
would pick up her hoop skirts and move as directed,
often revealing the scuffed Jellies she had worn that
day to school. A few weeks later there she would be,
transformed in *Diario Las Americas*, one of the morning battalion of smoldering fifteen-year-olds, each with
her arch, her fountain, her borrowed scenery, the gift

if not exactly the intention of the late George Merrick, who built the arches when he developed Coral Gables.

Neither the photographs of the Cuban *quinceañeras* nor the notes about the *coctel* at the Big Five were apt to appear in the newspapers read by Miami Anglos, nor, for that matter, was much information at all about the daily life of the Cuban majority. When, in the fall of 1986, Florida International University offered an evening course called "Cuban Miami: A Guide for Non-Cubans," the *Herald* sent a staff writer, who covered the classes as if from a distant beat. "Already I have begun to make some sense out of a culture that, while it totally surrounds us, has remained inaccessible and alien to me," the *Herald* writer was reporting by the end of the first meeting, and, by the end of the fourth: "What I see day to day in Miami, moving through mostly Anglo corridors of the community, are just small bits and pieces of that other world, the tip of something much larger than I'd imagined. . . . We may frequent the restaurants here, or wander into the occasional festival. But mostly we try to ignore Cuban Miami, even as we rub up against this teeming, incomprehensible presence."

Only thirteen people, including the *Herald* writer, turned up for the first meeting of "Cuban Miami: A Guide for Non-Cubans" (two more appeared at the second meeting, along with a security guard, because of telephone threats prompted by what the *Herald* writer called "somebody's twisted sense of national pride"), an enrollment which tended to suggest a certain willingness among non-Cubans to let Cuban Miami remain just that, Cuban, the "incomprehensible presence." In fact there had come to exist in South Florida two parallel cultures, separate but not exactly equal, a key distinction being that only one of the two, the Cuban, exhibited even a remote interest in the activities of the other. "The American community is not really aware of what is happening in the Cuban community," an exile banker named Luis Botifoll said in a 1983 *Herald* Sunday magazine piece about ten prominent local Cubans. "We are clannish, but at least we know who is who in the American establishment. They do not." About another of the ten Cubans featured in this piece, Jorge Mas Canosa, the *Herald* had this to say: "He is an advisor to U.S. Senators, a confidant of federal bureaucrats, a lobbyist for anti-Castro U.S. policies, a near unknown in Miami. When his political group sponsored a luncheon speech in Miami by Secretary of Defense Caspar Weinberger, almost none of the American business leaders attending had ever heard of their Cuban host."

The general direction of this piece, which appeared under the cover line "THE CUBANS: *They're ten of the most powerful men in Miami. Half the population doesn't know it*," was, as the *Herald* put it, "to challenge the widespread presumption that Miami's Cubans are not really Americans, that they are a foreign presence here, an exile community that is trying to turn South Florida into North Cuba. . . . The top ten are not separatists; they have achieved success in the most traditional ways. They are the solid, bedrock citizens, hard-working humanitarians who are role models for a community that seems determined to assimilate itself into American society."

This was interesting. It was written by one of the few Cubans then on the *Herald* staff, and yet it described, however unwittingly, the precise angle at which Miami Anglos and Miami Cubans were failing to connect: Miami Anglos were in fact interested in Cubans only to the extent that they could cast them as aspiring immigrants, "determined to assimilate," a "hard-working" minority not different in kind from other groups of resident aliens. (But had I met any Haitians, a number of Anglos asked when I said that I had been talking to Cubans.) Anglos (who were, significantly, referred to within the Cuban community as "Americans") spoke of cross-culturalization, and of what they believed to be a meaningful second-generation preference for hamburgers, and rock and roll. They spoke of "diversity," and of Miami's "Hispanic flavor," an approach in which 56 percent of the population was seen as decorative, like the Coral Gables arches.

Fixed as they were on this image of the melting pot, of immigrants fleeing a disruptive revolution to find a place in the American sun, Anglos did not on the whole understand that assimilation would be considered by most Cubans a doubtful goal at best. Nor did many Anglos understand that living in Florida was still at the deepest level construed by Cubans as a temporary condition, an accepted political option shaped by the continuing dream, if no longer the immediate expectation, of a vindicatory return. *El exilio* was for Cubans a ritual, a respected tradition. *La revolución* was also a ritual, a trope fixed in Cuban political rhetoric at least since José Martí, a concept broadly interpreted to mean reform, or progress, or even just change. Ramón Grau San Martín, the president of Cuba during the autumn of 1933 and again from 1944 until 1948, had presented himself as a revolutionary, as had his 1948 successor, Carlos Prío. Even Fulgencio Batista had entered Havana life calling for *la revolución*, and had later been accused of betraying it, even as Fidel Castro was now.

This was a process Cuban Miami understood, but Anglo Miami did not, remaining as it did arrestingly innocent of even the most general information about Cuba and Cubans. Miami Anglos, for example, still had trouble with Cuban names, and Cuban food. When the Cuban novelist Guillermo Cabrera Infante came from London to lecture at Miami-Dade Community College, he was referred to by several Anglo faculty members to whom I spoke as "Infante." Cuban food was widely seen not as a minute variation on that eaten throughout both the Caribbean and the Mediterranean but as "exotic," and full of garlic. A typical Thursday food section of the *Herald* included recipes for Broiled Lemon-Curry Cornish Game Hens, Chicken Tetrazzini, King Cake, Pimiento Cheese, Raisin Sauce for Ham, Sautéed Spiced Peaches, Shrimp Scampi, Easy Beefy Stir-Fry, and four ways to use dried beans ("Those cheap, humble beans that have long sustained the world's poor have become the trendy set's new pet"), none of them Cuban.

This was all consistent, and proceeded from the original construction, that of the exile as an immigration. There was no reason to be curious about Cuban food, because Cuban teenagers preferred hamburgers. There was no reason to get Cuban names right, because they were complicated, and would be simplified by the second generation, or even by the first. "Jorge L. Mas" was the way Jorge Más Canosa's business card read. "Raul Masvidal" was the way Raúl Masvidal y Jury ran for mayor of Miami. There was no reason to know about Cuban history, because history was what immigrants were fleeing. Even the revolution, the reason for the immigration, could be covered in a few broad strokes: "Batista," "Castro," "26 Julio," this last being the particular broad stroke that inspired the Miami Springs Holiday Inn, on July 26, 1985, the thirty-second anniversary of the day Fidel Castro attacked the Moncada Barracks and so launched his six-year struggle for power in Cuba, to run a bar special on Cuba Libres, thinking to attract local Cubans by commemorating their holiday. "It was a mistake," the manager said, besieged by outraged exiles. "The gentleman who did it is from Minnesota."

There was in fact no reason, in Miami as well as in Minnesota, to know anything at all about Cubans, since Miami Cubans were now, if not Americans, at least aspiring Americans, and worthy of Anglo attention to the exact extent that they were proving themselves, in the *Herald*'s words, "role models for a community that seems determined to assimilate itself into American society"; or, as Vice President George Bush put it in a 1986 Miami address to the Cuban American National Foundation, "the most eloquent testimony I know to the basic strength and success of America, as well as to the basic weakness and failure of Communism and Fidel Castro."

The use of this special lens, through which the exiles were seen as a tribute to the American system, a point scored in the battle of the ideologies, tended to be encouraged by those outside observers who dropped down from the northeast corridor for a look and a column or two. George Will, in *Newsweek*, saw Miami as "a new installment in the saga of America's absorptive capacity," and Southwest Eighth Street as the place where "these exemplary Americans," the seven Cubans who had been gotten together to brief him, "initiated a columnist to fried bananas and black-bean soup and other Cuban contributions to the tanginess of American life." George Gilder, in *The Wilson Quarterly*, drew pretty much the same lesson from Southwest Eighth Street, finding it "more effervescently thriving than its crushed prototype," by which he seemed to mean Havana. In fact Eighth Street was for George Gilder a street that seemed to "percolate with the forbidden commerce of the dying island to the south . . . the Refrescos Cawy, the Competidora and El Cuño cigarettes, the *guayaberas*, the Latin music pulsing from the storefronts, the pyramids of mangoes and tubers, gourds and plantains, the iced coconuts served with a straw, the new theaters showing the latest anti-Castro comedies."

There was nothing on this list, with the possible exception of the "anti-Castro comedies," that could not most days be found on Southwest Eighth Street, but the list was also a fantasy, and a particularly gringo fantasy, one in which Miami Cubans, who came from a culture which had represented western civilization in this hemisphere since before there was a United States of America, appeared exclusively as vendors of plantains, their native music "pulsing" behind them. There was in any such view of Miami Cubans an extraordinary element of condescension, and it was the very condescension shared by Miami Anglos, who were inclined to reduce the particular liveliness and sophistication of local Cuban life to a matter of shrines on the lawn and love potions in the *botánicas*, the primitive exotica of the tourist's Caribbean.

Cubans were perceived as most satisfactory when they appeared to most fully share the aspirations and manners of middle-class Americans, at the same time adding "color" to the city on appropriate occasions, for example at their *quinces* (the *quinces* were one aspect of Cuban life almost invariably mentioned by Anglos, who tended to present them as evidence of Cuban extravagance, *i.e.*, Cuban irresponsibility, or childishness), or on the day of the annual Calle Ocho Festival, when they could, according to the *Herald*, "samba" in the streets and stir up a paella for two thousand (10 cooks, 2,000 mussels, 220 pounds of lobster and 440 pounds of rice), using rowboat oars as spoons. Cubans were perceived as least satisfactory when they "acted clannish," "kept to themselves," "had their own ways," and, two frequent flash points, "spoke Spanish when they didn't need to" and "got political"; complaints, each of them, which suggested an Anglo view of what Cubans should be at significant odds with what Cubans were.

6

This question of language was curious. The sound of spoken Spanish was common in Miami, but it was also common in Los Angeles, and Houston, and even in the cities of the northeast. What was unusual about Spanish in Miami was not that it was so often spoken, but that it was so often heard: in, say, Los Angeles, Spanish remained a language only barely registered by the Anglo population, part of the ambient noise, the language spoken by the people who worked in the car wash and came to trim the trees and cleared the tables in restaurants. In Miami Spanish was spoken by the people who ate in the restaurants, the people who owned the cars and the trees, which made, on the socioauditory scale, a considerable difference. Exiles who felt isolated or declassed by language in New York or Los Angeles thrived in Miami. An entrepreneur who spoke no English could still, in Miami, buy, sell, negotiate, leverage assets, float bonds, and, if he were so inclined, attend galas twice a week, in black tie. "I have been after the *Herald* ten times to do a story about millionaires in Miami who do not speak more than two words in English," one prominent exile told me. " 'Yes' and 'no.' Those are the two words. They come here with five dollars in their pockets and without speaking another word of English they are millionaires."

The truculence a millionaire who spoke only two words of English might provoke among the less resourceful native citizens of a nominally American city was predictable, and manifested itself rather directly. In 1980, the year of Mariel, Dade County voters had approved a referendum requiring that county business be conducted exclusively in English. Notwithstanding the fact that this legislation was necessarily amended to exclude emergency medical and certain other services, and notwithstanding even the fact that many local meetings continued to be conducted in that unbroken alternation of Spanish and English which had become the local patois ("I will be in Boston on Sunday and desafortunadamente yo tengo un compromiso en Boston que no puedo romper y yo no podré estar con Vds.," read the minutes of a 1984 Miami City Commission meeting I had occasion to look up. "En espíritu, estaré, pero the other members of the commission I am sure are invited . . ."), the very existence of this referendum was seen by many as ground regained, a point made. By 1985 a St. Petersburg optometrist named Robert Melby was launching his third attempt in four years to have English declared the official language of the state of Florida, as it would be in 1986 of California. "I don't know why your legislators here are so, how should I put it?—spineless," Robert Melby complained about those South

Florida politicians who knew how to count. "No one down here seems to want to run with the issue."

Even among those Anglos who distanced themselves from such efforts, Anglos who did not perceive themselves as economically or socially threatened by Cubans, there remained considerable uneasiness on the matter of language, perhaps because the inability or the disinclination to speak English tended to undermine their conviction that assimilation was an ideal universally shared by those who were to be assimilated. This uneasiness had for example shown up repeatedly during the 1985 mayoralty campaign, surfacing at odd but apparently irrepressible angles. The winner of that contest, Xavier Suarez, who was born in Cuba but educated in the United States, was reported in a wire service story to speak, an apparently unexpected accomplishment, "flawless English."

A less prominent Cuban candidate for mayor that year had unsettled reporters at a televised "meet the candidates" forum by answering in Spanish the questions they asked in English. "For all I or my dumbstruck colleagues knew," the *Herald* political editor complained in print after this event, "he was reciting his high school's alma mater or the ten Commandments over and over again. The only thing I understood was the occasional *Cubano vota Cubano* he tossed in." It was noted by another *Herald* columnist that of the leading candidates, only one, Raul Masvidal, had a listed telephone number, but: ". . . if you call Masvidal's 661-0259 number on Kiaora Street in

Coconut Grove—during the day, anyway—you'd better speak Spanish. I spoke to two women there, and neither spoke enough English to answer the question of whether it was the candidate's number."

On the morning this last item came to my attention in the *Herald* I studied it for some time. Raul Masvidal was at that time the chairman of the board of the Miami Savings Bank and the Miami Savings Corporation. He was a former chairman of the Biscayne Bank, and a minority stockholder in the M Bank, of which he had been a founder. He was a member of the Board of Regents for the state university system of Florida. He had paid $600,000 for the house on Kiaora Street in Coconut Grove, buying it specifically because he needed to be a Miami resident (Coconut Grove is part of the city of Miami) in order to run for mayor, and he had sold his previous house, in the incorporated city of Coral Gables, for $1,100,000. The Spanish words required to find out whether the number listed for the house on Kiaora Street was in fact the candidate's number would have been roughly these: *"Es la casa de Raúl Masvidal?"* The answer might have been *"Sí,"* or the answer might have been *"No."* It seemed to me that there must be very few people working on daily newspapers along the southern borders of the United States who would consider this exchange entirely out of reach, and fewer still who would not accept it as a commonplace of American domestic life that daytime telephone calls to middle-class urban households will frequently be answered by women who speak Spanish.

Something else was at work in this item, a real resistance, a balkiness, a coded version of the same message Dade County voters had sent when they decreed that their business be done only in English. WILL THE LAST AMERICAN TO LEAVE MIAMI PLEASE BRING THE FLAG, the famous bumper stickers had read the year of Mariel. "It was the last American stronghold in Dade County," the owner of Gator Kicks Longneck Saloon, out where Southwest Eight Street runs into the Everglades, had said after he closed the place for good the night of Super Bowl Sunday, 1986. "Fortunately or unfortunately, I'm not alone in my inability," a *Herald* columnist named Charles Whited had written a week or so later, in a column about not speaking Spanish. "A good many Americans have left Miami because they want to live someplace where everybody speaks one language: theirs." In this context the call to the house on Kiaora Street in Coconut Grove which did or did not belong to Raul Masvidal appeared not as a statement of literal fact but as shorthand, a glove thrown down, a stand, a cry from the heart of a beleaguered raj.

7

O_N the whole the members of the beleaguered raj and the 56 percent of the population whose affairs they continued to believe they directed did not see politics on the same canvas, which tended to complicate the Anglo complaint about the way in which Cubans "got political."

Every election in the city of Miami produces its share of rumors involving the *Herald*, and last Tuesday's mayoral runoff between Raul Masvidal and Xavier Suarez produced one that I think I'll have bronzed and hang on my office wall. It was *that* bizarre.

Political Editor Tom Fiedler reported it in his column on Thursday. The previous day, Mr. Suarez was sworn in as mayor after readily defeating Mr. Masvidal, whom this newspaper had recommended, in the runoff. Tom wrote that "the rumor going around Little Havana is that the *Herald* really preferred Suarez the best and only used Masvidal as a feint. Follow this reasoning closely, now: because the newspaper knows that its endorsement actually hurts candidates in Little Havana, it endorsed Masvidal with the knowledge that Suarez would be the beneficiary of a backlash. Thus, according to this rationale, the *Herald* actually got what it wanted. Clever, huh?"

I wish I knew where behind the looking glass the authors of these contortions reside. I'd like to meet them, really I would. Maybe if we chatted I could begin to understand the thought processes that make them see up as down, black as white, alpha as omega. Or maybe I simply would be left where I am now: scratching my head and chortling in baffled amusement.

> —Jim Hampton, Editor, the *Miami Herald*, November 17, 1985

Miami Anglos continued, as the editor of the *Herald* did, to regard the density and febrility of exile political life with "baffled amusement." They continued, as the editor of the *Herald* did, to find that life "bizarre." They thought of politics exactly the way most of their elected representatives thought of politics, not as the very structure of everything they did but as a specific and usually programmatic kind of activity: an election, a piece of legislation, the deals made and the trade-offs extracted during the course of the campaign or the legislative markup. Any more general notions tended to be amorphous, the detritus of a desultory education in the confident latitudes: politics were part of "civics," one of the "social studies," something taught with audiovisual aids and having as its goal the promotion of good citizenship.

Politics, in other words, remained a "subject," an assortment of maxims once learned and still available to be learned by those not blessed with American birth, which may have been why, on those infrequent occasions when the city's parallel communities contrived an opportunity to express their actual feelings about each other, Miami Anglos tended unveeringly toward the didactic. On March 7, 1986, a group called the South Florida Peace Coalition applied for and received a Miami police permit authorizing a demonstration, scheduled for a Saturday noon some two weeks later at the Torch of Friendship monument on Biscayne Boulevard, against American aid to the Nicaraguan contras. Since the cause of the Nicaraguan contras was one with which many Miami Cubans had come to identify their most febrile hopes and fears, the prospect of such a demonstration was not likely to go unremarked upon, nor did it: in due course, after what was apparently a general sounding of the alarm on local Cuban radio, a second police permit was applied for and issued, this one to Andres Nazario Sargen, the executive director of Alpha 66, one of the most venerable of the exile action groups and one which had regularly claimed, ever since what had appeared to be its original encouragement in 1962 by the CIA, to be running current actions against the government of Cuba.

This second permit authorized a counterdemonstration, intended not so much to show support for the contras, which in context went without saying, as to show opposition to those Anglos presumed to be working for hemispheric communism. "We took it as a challenge," Andres Nazario Sargen said of the original permit and its holders. "They know very well they are defending a communist regime, and that hurts the Cuban exile's sensibility." That the permits would allow the South Florida Peace Coalition demonstration and the Alpha 66 counterdemonstration to take place at exactly the same time and within a few yards of each other was a point defended by Miami police, the day before the scheduled events, as a "manpower" decision, a question of not wanting to "split resources." "With the number of police officers who will be there," a police spokesman was quoted as saying, "someone would have to be foolish to try anything."

This was not an assessment which suggested a particularly close reading, over the past twenty-five years, of either Alpha 66 or Andres Nazario Sargen, and I was not unduly surprised, on the Sunday morning after the fact, to find the front page of the *Herald* given over to double headlines (DEMONSTRATIONS TURN UGLY and VIOLENCE MARS PRO-CONTRA PROTEST) and a four-color photograph showing a number of exiles brandishing Cuban and American flags as they burned the placards abandoned by the routed South Florida Peace Coalition. It appeared that many eggs had been hurled, and some rocks. It appeared that at least one onion had been hurled, hitting the president of the Dade County Young Democrats, who later expressed his thoughts on the matter by describing himself as "an eleventh-generation American."

It appeared, moreover, that these missiles had been

hurled in just one direction, that of the South Florida Peace Coalition demonstrators, a group of about two hundred which included, besides the president of the Dade County Young Democrats, some state and local legislators, some members of the American Friends Service Committee, a few people passing out leaflets bearing the name of the Revolutionary Communist Party, one schoolteacher who advised the *Herald* that she was there because "Americans need to reclaim Miami from these foreigners," and, the most inflammatory cut of all for the Alpha 66 demonstrators on the other side of the metal police barricades, at least one Cuban, a leader of the Antonio Maceo Brigade, a heretical exile group founded in the mid-seventies to sponsor student visits to Cuba.

From noon of that Saturday until about three, when a riot squad was called and the South Florida Peace Coalition physically extracted from the fray, the police had apparently managed to keep the Alpha 66 demonstrators on the Alpha 66 side of the barricades. The two hundred Peace Coalition demonstrators had apparently spent those three hours listening to speeches and singing folk songs. The two thousand Alpha 66 demonstrators had apparently spent the three hours trying to rush the barricades, tangling with police, and shouting down the folksingers with chants of *"Comunismo no, Democracia sí,"* and *"Rusia no, Reagan sí."* The mayor of Miami, Xavier Suarez, had apparently stayed on the Alpha 66 side of the barricades, at one point speaking from the back of a Mazda pickup, a technique he later described in a letter to the *Herald* as "mingling with the people and expressing my own philosophical agreement with their ideas— as well as my disagreement with the means by which some would implement those ideas," and also as "an effective way to control the crowd."

"Unfortunately, they have the right to be on the other side of the street" was what he apparently said at the time, from the back of the Mazda pickup. "I'm sure you've all looked clearly to see who is on that side, senators and representatives included, and surely some members of Marxist groups." This method of crowd control notwithstanding, nothing much seemed actually to have happened that Saturday afternoon at the Torch of Friendship (only one demonstrator had been arrested, only one required hospital treatment), but the fevers of the moment continued for some weeks to induce a certain exhortatory delirium in the pages of the *Herald*. Statements were framed, and letters to the editor written, mostly along the preceptive lines favored by the Anglo community.

"I was raised to believe that the right to peaceful dissent was vital to our freedoms," one such letter read, from a woman who noted that she had been present at the Peace Coalition demonstration but had "fortunately" been "spared the vocal vituperation—as it was totally in the Spanish language." "Apparently," she continued, "some in the Cuban community do not recognize my right. . . . Evidently, their definition of human rights is not the same as that of most native-born Americans. It is as simple as that. No, my Cuban brothers and sisters, this is not the American way. Shame!"

Voltaire was quoted, somewhat loosely (" 'I disagree with what you say, but I will defend to the death your right to say it' "), and even Wendell Willkie, the inscription on whose grave marker (" 'Because we are generous with our freedom, we share our rights with those who disagree with us' ") was said to be "our American creed, as spelled out in the Constitution." One correspondent mentioned how "frightening" it was to realize "that although we live in a democracy that guarantees the right of free speech, when we exercise this right we can be physically attacked by a group of people whom we have given refuge here in our country."

The subtext here, that there were some people who belonged in Miami and other people who did not, became, as the letters mounted, increasingly explicit, taking on finally certain aspects of a crusade. "Perhaps," another correspondent suggested, taking the point a step further, "it is time for a change of venue to countries in which they may vent their spleen at risk only to the governments they oppose and themselves." A *Herald* columnist, Carl Hiaasen, put the matter even more flatly: "They have come to the wrong country," he wrote about those pro-contra demonstrators who had that Saturday afternoon attacked a young man named David Camp, "a carpenter and stagehand who was born here, and has always considered himself patriotic . . . They need to go someplace where they won't have to struggle so painfully with the concept of free speech, or the right to dissent. Someplace where the names of Paine and Jefferson have no meaning, where folks wouldn't know the Bill of Rights if it was stapled to their noses."

If this native reduction of politics to a Frank Capra movie was not an approach which provided much of a libretto for the tropical Ring of exile and conspiracy that had been Cuban political experience, neither had the Cubans arrived in Miami equipped with much instinctive feeling for the native way. Miami Cubans were not the heirs to a tradition in which undue effort had been spent defining the rights and responsibilities of "good citizens," nor to one in which loosely organized democracies on the American model were widely admired. They were the heirs instead to the Spanish Inquisition, and after that to a tradition of anti-Americanism so sturdy that it had often been for Cubans a motive force. "It is my duty," José Martí had written to a friend in May of 1895, a few days before he was killed on his white horse fighting for the independence of Cuba at Dos Ríos, "to prevent, through the independence of Cuba, the U.S.A. from spreading over the West Indies and falling with added weight upon other lands of Our America. All I have done up to now and shall do hereafter is to that end. . . . I know the Monster, because I have lived in its lair—and my weapon is only the slingshot of David."

From within this matrix, which was essentially autocratic, Miami Cubans looked at the merely accidental in American life and found a design, often sinister. They looked at what amounted to Anglo indifference (on the question, say, of which of two Cubans, neither of whom could be expected to recall the Hurricane of 1926 or the opening of the Dixie Highway, was to be mayor of Miami) and divined a conspiratorial intention. They looked at American civil rights and saw civil disorder. They had their own ideas about how order should be maintained, even in the lair of the Monster that was the United States. "All underaged children will not be allowed to leave their homes by themselves," one Cuban candidate in the 1985 Miami mayoralty campaign promised to ensure if elected. "They should always be accompanied by an adult, with parents or guardians being responsible for compliance with the law." Another Cuban candidate in the same election, General Manuel Benítez, who had been at one time chief of the Batista security forces, promised this: ". . . you can rest assured that within six months there will be no holdups, life in general will be protected and stores will be able to open their doors without fear of robberies or murders. . . . A powerful force of security guards, the county school personnel, teachers, professionals, retirees, Boy Scouts and church people will all take part in a program of citizen education and in the constant fight against evil and immorality."

"Unfortunately," as the winning candidate in that campaign, Mayor Xavier Suarez, had said of the Peace Coalition demonstrators at the Torch of Friendship, "they have the right to be on the other side of the street." That this was a right devised to benefit those who would subvert civil order was, for many Cubans, a given, because this was a community in which nothing could be inadvertent, nothing without its place in a larger, usually hostile, scheme. The logic was close, even claustrophobic. That the *Herald* should have run, on the 1985 anniversary of the Bay of Pigs, a story about Canadian and Italian tourists vacationing on what had been the invasion beaches (RESORT SELLS SUN, FUN—IN CUBA: TOPLESS BATHERS FROLIC AS HAVANA TRIES HAND AT TOURISM) was, in this view, not just a minor historical irony, not just an arguably insensitive attempt to find a news peg for a twenty-four-year-old annual story, but a calculated affront to the Cuban community, "a slap," I was repeatedly told, "in the face." That the *Herald* should have run, a few weeks before, a story suggesting a greater availability of consumer goods in Cuba (FREE MARKETS ALLOW HAVANA TO SPIFF UP) not only sealed the affront but indicated that it was systematic, directed by Washington and signaling a rapprochement between the Americans and Havana, the imminence of which was a fixed idea among Miami Cubans.

Fixed ideas about Americans seemed, among Miami Cubans, general. Americans, I was frequently told, never touched one another, nor did they argue. Americans did not share the attachment to family which characterized Cuban life. Americans did not share the attachment to *patria* which characterized Cuban life. Americans placed undue importance on being on time. Americans were undereducated. Americans, at one and the same time, acted exclusively in their own interests and failed to see their own interests, not only because they were undereducated but because they were by temperament "naive," a people who could live and die without ever understanding those nuances of conspiracy and allegiance on which, in the Cuban view, the world turned.

Americans, above all, lacked "passion," which was the central failing from which most of these other national peculiarities flowed. If I wanted evidence that Americans lacked passion, I was advised repeatedly, I had only to consider their failure to appreciate *la lucha*. If I wanted further evidence that Americans lacked passion, I had only to turn on a television set and watch Ted Koppel's "Nightline," a program on which, I was told a number of times, it was possible to observe Americans "with very opposing points of view" talking "completely without passion," "without any gestures at all," and "seemingly without any idea in the world of conspiring against each other, despite being totally opposed."

This repeated reference to "Nightline" was arresting. At the end of a day or an evening in Miami I would look through my notes and find the references underlined and boxed in my notebook, with arrows, and the notation, "Ch.: NIGHTLINE???" The mode of discourse favored by Ted Koppel (it was always, for reasons I never discerned, Ted Koppel, no one else) and his guests seemed in fact so consistent a source of novelty and derision among the Cubans to whom I spoke in Miami that I began to see these mentions of

"Nightline" as more shorthand, the Cuban version of the Anglo telephone call to the house on Kiaora Street in Coconut Grove which did or did not belong to Raul Masvidal, another glove thrown down, another stand; the code which indicated that the speaker, like José Martí, knew the Monster, and did not mean to live easily in its lair.

"Let those who desire a secure homeland conquer it," José Martí also wrote. "Let those who do not conquer it live under the whip and in exile, watched over like wild animals, cast from one country to another, concealing the death of their souls with a beggar's smile from the scorn of free men." The humiliation of the continuing exile was what the Monster, lacking passion, did not understand. It was taken for granted in this continuing exile that the Monster, lacking passion or understanding, could be utilized. It was also taken for granted in this continuing exile that the Monster, lacking passion or understanding, could not be trusted. "We must attempt to strengthen the non-Batista democratic anti-Castro forces in exile," a John F. Kennedy campaign statement had declared in the course of working up an issue against Richard Nixon in 1960. "We cannot have the United States walk away from one of the greatest moral challenges in postwar history," Ronald Reagan had declared in the course of working up support for the Nicaraguan freedom fighters in 1985.

"We have seen that movie before," one prominent exile had said to me about the matter of the United

States not, as Ronald Reagan had put it, walking away from the Nicaraguan freedom fighters. Here between the mangrove swamp and the barrier reef was an American city largely populated by people who believed that the United States had walked away before, had betrayed them at the Bay of Pigs and later, with consequences we have since seen. Here between the swamp and the reef was an American city populated by people who also believed that the United States would betray them again, in Honduras and in El Salvador and in Nicaragua, betray them at all the barricades of a phantom war they had once again taken not as the projection of another Washington abstraction but as their own struggle, *la lucha, la causa,* with consequences we have not yet seen.

THREE

8

"**D**ON'T forget that we have a disposal problem" is what Arthur M. Schlesinger, Jr., tells us that Allen Dulles said on March 11, 1961, by way of warning John F. Kennedy about the possible consequences of aborting the projected Cuban invasion and cutting loose what the CIA knew to be a volatile and potentially vengeful asset, the 2506 Brigade. What John F. Kennedy was said to have said, four weeks later, to Arthur M. Schlesinger, Jr., is this: "If we have to get rid of these 800 men, it is much better to dump them in Cuba than in the United States, especially if that is where they want to go." This is dialogue recalled by someone without much ear for it, and the number of men involved in the invasion force was closer to fifteen hundred than to eight hundred, but the core of it, the "dump them in Cuba" construction, has an authentic ring, as does "disposal problem" itself. Over the years since the publication of *A Thousand Days* I had read the chapter in which these two lines appear several times, but only after I had spent time in Miami did I begin to see them as curtain lines, or as the cannon which the protagonist brings onstage in the first act so that it may be fired against him in the third.

"I would say that John F. Kennedy is still the number two most hated man in Miami," Raul Masvidal said to me one afternoon, not long after he had announced his candidacy for mayor, in a cool and immaculate office on the top floor of one of the Miami banks in which he has an interest. Raul Masvidal, who was born in Havana in 1942, would seem in many ways a model for what both Anglo Miami and the rest of the United States like to see as Cuban assimilation. He was named by both Cubans and non-Cubans in a 1983 *Miami Herald* poll as the most powerful Cuban in Miami. He received the endorsement of the *Herald* in his campaign to become mayor of Miami, the election he ultimately lost to Xavier Suarez. He was, at the time we spoke, one of two Cuban members (the other being Armando Codina, a Miami entrepreneur and member of the advisory board of the Southeast First National Bank) of The Non-Group, an unofficial and extremely private organization which had been called the shadow government of South Florida and included among its thirty-eight members, who met once a month for dinner at one another's houses or clubs, the ownership or top management of Knight-Ridder, Eastern Airlines, Arvida Disney, Burdines, the Miami Dolphins, and the major banks and utilities.

"Castro is of course the number one most hated," Raul Masvidal added. "Then Kennedy. The entire Kennedy family." He opened and closed a leather folder, the only object on his marble desk, then aligned it with the polished edge of the marble. On the wall behind him hung a framed poster with the legend, in English, YOU HAVE NOT CONVERTED A MAN BECAUSE YOU HAVE SILENCED HIM, a sentiment so outside the thrust of local Cuban thinking that it lent the office an aspect of having been dressed exclusively for visits from what Cubans sometimes call, with a slight ironic edge, the mainstream population.

"Something I did which involved Ted Kennedy became very controversial here," Raul Masvidal said then. "Jorge asked me to contact Senator Kennedy." He was talking about Jorge Mas Canosa, the Miami engineering contractor (the "advisor to U.S. Senators," "confidant of federal bureaucrats," "lobbyist for anti-Castro U.S. policies" and "near unknown in Miami," as the *Herald* had described him a few years before) who had been, through the Washington office of the Cuban American National Foundation and its companion PAC, the National Coalition for a Free Cuba, instrumental in the lobbying for Radio Martí. "To see if we could get him to reverse his position on Radio Martí. We needed Kennedy to change his vote, to give that bill the famous luster. I did that. And the Cubans here took it as if it had been an attempt to make peace with the Kennedys."

The man who had been accused of attempting to make peace with the Kennedys arrived in this country in 1960, when he was eighteen. He enrolled at the University of Miami, then took two semesters off to train with the 2506 for the Bay of Pigs. After the 1962 Cuban missile crisis, which was then and is still perceived in Miami as another personal betrayal on the part of John F. Kennedy, Raul Masvidal again dropped out of the University of Miami, this time to join a unit of Cubans recruited by the United States Army for training at Fort Knox, Kentucky, part of what Theodore C. Sorensen, in *Kennedy*, recalled in rather soft focus as a "special arrangement" under which Bay of Pigs veterans "were quietly entering the American armed forces."

This seems to have been, even through the filter offered by diarists of the Kennedy administration, a gray area. Like other such ad hoc attempts to neutralize the 2506, the recruitment program involved, if not outright deception, a certain encouragement of self-deception, an apparent willingness to allow those Cubans who "were quietly entering the American armed forces" to do so under the misapprehension that the United States was in fact preparing to invade Cuba. Sentences appear to have been left unfinished, and hints dropped. Possibilities appear to have been floated, and not exclusively, as it has become the convention in this kind of situation to suggest, by some uncontrollable element in the field, some rogue agent. "President Kennedy came to the Orange Bowl and made us a promise," Jorge Mas Canosa, who is also a veteran of the 2506, repeated insistently to me one morning, his voice rising in the retelling of what has become for Miami a primal story. "December. Nineteen sixty-two. What he said turned out to be another—I won't say deception, let us call it a misconception—another misconception on the part of President Kennedy."

Jorge Mas Canosa had drawn the words "President" and "Kennedy" out, inflecting all syllables with equal emphasis. This was the same Jorge Mas Canosa who had enlisted Raul Masvidal in the effort to secure the luster of the Kennedy name for Radio Martí, the Jorge Mas Canosa who had founded the Cuban American National Foundation and was one of those funding its slick offices overlooking the Potomac in Georgetown; the Jorge Mas Canosa who had become so much a figure in Washington that it was sometimes hard to catch up with him in Miami. I had driven finally down the South Dixie Highway that morning to meet him at his main construction yard, the cramped office of which was decorated with a LONG LIVE FREE GRENADA poster and framed photographs of Jorge Mas Canosa with Ronald Reagan and Jorge Mas Canosa with Jeane Kirkpatrick and Jorge Mas Canosa with Paula Hawkins. "And at the Orange Bowl he was given the flag," Jorge Mas Canosa continued. "The flag the invasion forces had taken to Playa Girón. And he took this flag in his hands and he promised that he would return it to us in a free Havana. And he called on us to join the United States armed forces. To get training. And try again."

This particular effort to get the cannon offstage foundered, as many such efforts foundered, on the familiar shoal of Washington hubris. In this instance the hubris took the form of simultaneously underestimating the exiles' distrust of the United States and overestimating their capacity for self-deception, which, although considerable, was tempered always by a rather more extensive experience in the politics of conspiracy than the Kennedy administration's own. The exiles had not, once they put it together that the point of the exercise was to keep them occupied, served easily. Jorge Mas Canosa, who had been sent to Fort Benning, had stayed only long enough to finish OCS, then resigned his commission and returned to Miami. At Fort Knox, according to Raul Masvidal, there had been, "once it became evident that the United States and Russia had reached an agreement and the United States had no intention of invading Cuba," open rebellion.

"A lot of things happened," Raul Masvidal said. "For example we had a strike, which was unheard of for soldiers. One day we just decided we were going to remain in our barracks for a few days. They threatened us with all kinds of things. But at that point we didn't care much for the threats." A representative of the Kennedy White House had finally been dispatched to Fort Knox to try to resolve the situation, and a deal had been struck, a renegotiated "special arrangement," under which the exiles agreed to end their strike in return for an immediate transfer to Fort Jackson, South Carolina (they had found Kentucky, they said, too cold), and an almost immediate discharge. At this point Raul Masvidal went back to the University of Miami, to parking cars at the Everglades Hotel, and to the more fluid strategies of CIA/ Miami, which was then running, through a front operation on the south campus of the University of Miami called Zenith Technological Services and code-named JM/WAVE, a kind of action about which everybody in Miami and nobody in Washington seemed to know.

"I guess during that period I was kind of a full-time student and part-time warrior," Raul Masvidal had recalled the afternoon we spoke. "In those days the CIA had these infiltration teams in the Florida Keys, and they ran sporadic missions to Cuba." These training camps in the Keys, which appear to have been simultaneously run by the CIA and, in what was after the Cuban missile crisis a further convolution of the disposal problem, periodically raided by the FBI, do not much figure in the literature of the Kennedy administration. Theodore C. Sorensen, in *Kennedy*, mentioned "a crackdown by Federal authorities on the publicity-seeking Cuban refugee groups who conducted hit-and-run raids on Cuban ports and shipping," further distancing the "publicity-seeking Cuban refugee groups" from the possessive plural of the White House by adding that they damaged "little other than our efforts to persuade the Soviets to leave." Arthur M. Schlesinger, Jr., elided this Miami action altogether in *A Thousand Days*, an essentially antihistorical work in which the entire matter of the Cuban exiles is seen to have resolved itself on an inspirational note in December of 1962, when Jacqueline Kennedy stood at the Orange Bowl before the Bay of Pigs veterans, 1,113 of whom had just returned from imprisonment in Cuba, and said, in Spanish, that she wanted her son to be "a man at least half as brave as the members of Brigade 2506." In his more complex reconsideration of the period, *Robert Kennedy and His Times*, Schlesinger did deal with the Miami action, but with so profound a queasiness as to suggest that the question of whether the United States government had or had not been involved with it ("But had CIA been up to its old tricks?") remained obscure, as if unknowable.

Such accounts seem, in Miami, where an impressive amount of the daily business of the city is carried on by men who speak casually of having run missions for the CIA, remote to the point of the delusional. According to reports published in 1975 and 1976 and prompted by hearings before the Church committee, the Senate Select Committee to Study Governmental Operations with Respect to Intelligence Operations, the CIA's JM/WAVE station on the University of Miami campus was by 1962 the largest CIA installation, outside Langley, in the world, and one of the largest employers in the state of Florida. There were said to have been at JM/WAVE headquarters between 300 and 400 case officers from the CIA's clandestine services branch. Each case officer was said to have run between four and ten Cuban "principal agents," who were referred to in code as "amots." Each principal agent was said to have run in turn between ten and thirty "regular agents," again mainly exiles.

The arithmetic here is impressive. Even the minimum figures, 300 case officers each running 4 principal agents who in turn ran 10 regular agents, yield 12,000 regular agents. The maximum figures yield 120,000 regular agents, each of whom might be pre-

sumed to have contacts of his own. There were, all
operating under the JM/WAVE umbrella, flotillas of
small boats. There were mother ships, disguised as
merchant vessels, what an unidentified CIA source
described to the *Herald* as "the third largest navy in
the western hemisphere." There was the CIA's Miami
airline, Southern Air Transport, acquired in 1960 and
subsequently financed through its holding company,
Actus Technology Inc., and through another CIA
holding company, the Pacific Corporation, with more
than $16.7 million in loans from the CIA's Air Amer-
ica and an additional $6.6 million from the Manufac-
turers Hanover Trust Company. There were hundreds
of pieces of Miami real estate, residential bungalows
maintained as safe houses, waterfront properties maintained as safe harbors. There were, besides the phantom "Zenith Technological Services" that was JM/
WAVE headquarters itself, fifty-four other front businesses, providing employment and cover and various
services required by JM/WAVE operations. There
were CIA boat shops. There were CIA gun shops.
There were CIA travel agencies and there were CIA
real-estate agencies and there were CIA detective agencies.

Anyone who spent any time at all on the street in
Miami during the early 1960s, then, was likely to have
had dealings with the CIA, to have known what actions were being run, to have known who was running them, and for whom. Among Cubans of his generation in Miami, Raul Masvidal was perhaps most
unusual in that he did not actually run the missions

himself. "I was more an assistant to the person who was running the program," he had said the day we talked. "Helping with the logistics. Making sure the people got fed and had the necessary weapons. It was a frustrating time, because you could see the pattern right away. The pattern was for a decline in activity toward Castro. We were just being kept busy. For two reasons. One reason was that it provided a certain amount of intelligence in which the CIA was interested."

Raul Masvidal is wary, almost impassive. He speaks carefully, in the even cadences of American management, the cadences of someone who received a degree in international business at Thunderbird, the American Graduate School of International Management in Arizona, and had been by the time he was thirty a vice president of Citibank in New York and Madrid, and this was one of the few occasions during our conversation when he allowed emotion to enter his voice. "The other reason," he said, "was that it was supposed to keep people in Miami thinking that something was being done. The fact that there were a few Cubans running around Miami saying that they were being trained, that they were running missions—well, it kept up a few hopes." Raul Masvidal paused. "So I guess that was important to the CIA," he said then. "To try to keep people here from facing the very hard and very frustrating fact that they were not going home because their strongest and best ally had made a deal. Behind their backs."

Bottom soundings are hard to come by here. We

are talking about 1963, the year which ended in the death of John F. Kennedy. It was a year described by Arthur M. Schlesinger, Jr., as one in which "the notion of invading Cuba had been dead for years" (since the notion of invading Cuba had demonstrably not been dead as recently as April of 1961, the "for years" is interesting on its face, and suggestive of the way in which Washington's perception of time expands and contracts with its agenda); a year in which, in the wake of the missile crisis and John F. Kennedy's 1962 agreement not to invade Cuba, the administration's anti-Castro policy had been "drastically modified" and in which the White House was in fact, as Schlesinger put it, "drifting toward accommodation." It was a year in which the official and well-publicized Washington policy toward Miami exile operations was one of unequivocal discouragement and even prosecution, a year of repeated exile arrests and weapons seizures; a year that was later described by the chief of station for JM/WAVE, in testimony before the Church committee, as one in which "the whole apparatus of government, Coast Guard, Customs, Immigration and Naturalization, FBI, CIA, were working together to try to keep these operations from going to Cuba." (The chief of station for JM/WAVE in 1963 happened to be Theodore Shackley, who left Miami in 1965, spent from 1966 until 1972 as political officer and chief of station in Vientiane and Saigon, and turned up in 1987 in the Tower Commission report, meeting on page B-3 in Hamburg with Manucher Ghorbanifar and with the former head of SAVAK counterespionage; discussing on page B-11 the hostage problem over lunch with Michael Ledeen.)

On the one hand "the whole apparatus of government" did seem to be "working together to try to keep these operations from going to Cuba," and on the other hand the whole apparatus of government seemed not to be doing this. There was still, it turned out, authorized CIA funding for such "autonomous operations" (a concept devised by Walt Whitman Rostow at the State Department) as the exile action group JURE, or Junta Revolucionaria Cubana, an "autonomous operation" being an operation, according to guidelines summarized in a CIA memorandum, with which the United States, "if ever charged with complicity," would deny having anything to do. "Autonomous operations" were, it turned out, part of the "track two" approach, which, whatever it meant in theory, meant for example in practice that JURE could, on "track two," request and receive explosives and grenades from the CIA even as, on track one, JURE was being investigated for possession of illegal firearms by the FBI and the INS.

"Track two" and "autonomous operations" were of course Washington phrases, phrases from the special vocabulary of Special Groups and Standing Groups and "guidelines" and "approaches," words from a language in which deniability was built into the grammar, and as such may or may not have had a different meaning, or any meaning, in 1963 in Miami, where deniability had become in many ways the very opposite of the point. In a CIA review of various attempts between 1960 and 1963 to assassinate Fidel Castro (which were "merely one aspect of the overall active effort to overthrow the regime," in other words not exactly a third track), an internal report prepared in 1967 by the Inspector General of the CIA and declassified in 1978 for release to the House Select Committee on Assassinations, there appears, on the matter of Washington language, this instructive reflection:

> . . . There is a third point, which was not directly made by any of those we interviewed, but which emerges clearly from the interviews and from reviews of files. The point is that of frequent resort to synecdoche—the mention of a part when the whole is to be understood, or vice versa. Thus, we encounter repeated references to phrases such as "disposing of Castro," which may be read in the narrow, literal sense of assassinating him, when it is intended that it be read in the broader, figurative sense of dislodging the Castro regime. Reversing the coin, we find people speaking vaguely of "doing something about Castro" when it is clear that what they have specifically in mind is killing him. In a situation wherein those speaking may not have actually meant what they seemed to say or may not have said what they actually meant, they should not be surprised if their oral shorthand is interpreted differently than was intended.

In the superimposition of the Washington dreamwork on that of Miami there has always been room, in other words, for everyone to believe what they need to believe. Arthur M. Schlesinger, Jr., in *Robert Kennedy and His Times*, finally went so far as to conclude that the CIA had during 1963 in Miami continued to wage what he still preferred to call "its private war against Castro," or had "evidently" done so, "despite," as he put it, in a clause that suggests the particular angle of deflection in the superimposition, "the lack of Special Group authorization." Asked at a press conference in May of 1963 whether either the CIA or the White House was supporting exile paramilitary operations, John F. Kennedy said this: "We may well be . . . well, none that I am familiar with . . . I don't think as of today that we are." What James Angleton, who was then chief of counterintelligence for the CIA, was later quoted as having said about the year 1963 in Miami, and about what the CIA was or was not doing, with or without Special Group authorization, was this: "The concept of Miami was correct. In a Latino area, it made sense to have a base in Miami for Latin American problems, as an extension of the desk. If it had been self-contained, then it would have had the quality of being a foreign base of sorts. It was a novel idea. But it got out of hand, it became a power unto itself. And when the target diminishes, it's very difficult for a bureaucracy to adjust. What do you do with your personnel? We owed a deep obligation to the men in Miami."

In Washington in 1962, according to a footnote in *Robert Kennedy and His Times*, "the regular Special

Group—[Maxwell] Taylor, McGeorge Bundy, Alexis Johnson, [Roswell] Gilpatric, [Lyman] Lemnitzer and [John] McCone—would meet at two o'clock every Thursday afternoon. When its business was finished, Robert Kennedy would arrive, and it would expand into the Special Group (CI). At the end of the day, Cuba would become the subject, and the group, with most of the same people, would metamorphose into Special Group (Augmented)." That was the context in which those people with the most immediate interest in the policy of the United States toward Cuba appear, during the years of the Kennedy administration, to have been talking in Washington. This was the context in which those people with the same interest during the same years appear, according to testimony later given before the Church committee by the 1963 chief of station for JM/WAVE, to have been talking in Miami: " 'Assassination' was part of the ambience of that time . . . nobody could be involved in Cuban operations without having had some sort of discussion at some time with some Cuban who said . . . the way to create a revolution is to shoot Fidel and Raúl . . . so the fact that somebody would talk about assassination just wasn't anything really out of the ordinary at that time."

What John F. Kennedy actually said when he held the 2506 flag in his hands at the Orange Bowl on December 29, 1962, was this: "I can assure you that this flag will be returned to this brigade in a free Havana." How Theodore C. Sorensen described this was as "a

supposed Kennedy promise for a second invasion."
How Arthur M. Schlesinger, Jr., described it was
as "a promise," but one "not in the script," a promise
made "in the emotion of the day." What Jorge Mas
Canosa said about it, that morning in the office with
the LONG LIVE FREE GRENADA poster and the framed
photographs of figures from yet another administration, the office in the construction yard forty minutes
down the South Dixie Highway, a forty-minute drive
down a flat swamp of motor home rentals and discount water-bed sales and boat repairs and bird and
reptile sales and Midas Mufflers and Radio Shacks, was
this: "I remember that later some people here made a
joke about President Kennedy and that promise." Jorge
Mas Canosa had again drawn out the syllables, *Pres-
ee-dent Ken-ned-ee*, and I listened closely, because,
during a considerable amount of time spent listening
to exiles in Miami talk about the promise John F. Kennedy made at the Orange Bowl, I had not before
heard anything approaching a joke. "The joke," Jorge
Mas Canosa said, "was that the 'Free Havana' he meant
was a bar by that name here in Miami."

9

To spend time in Miami is to acquire a certain fluency in cognitive dissonance. What Allen Dulles called the disposal problem is what Miami calls *la lucha*. One man's loose cannon is another's freedom fighter, or, in the local phrase, man of action, or man of valor. "This is a thing for men of valor, not for weaklings like you," an exile named Miriam Arocena had told the *Miami Herald* reporter who tried to interview her after the arrest of her husband, Eduardo Arocena, who was finally convicted, in a series of trials which ended a few days before the Bay of Pigs twenty-fourth anniversary observances at the 2506 bungalow and at the Martyrs of Girón monument and at the chapel which faces Cuba, of seventy-one federal counts connected with bombings in New York and Miami and with the 1980 assassination in New York of Félix García Rodríguez, an attaché at the Cuban mission to the United Nations, as well as with the attempted assassination the same year of Raúl Roa Kouri, at that time the Cuban ambassador to the United Nations.

The Florida bombings in question had taken place, between 1979 and 1983, at the Mexican consulate in Miami, at the Venezuelan consulate in Miami, and at various Miami businesses rumored in the exile community to have had dealings with, or sympathy for, or perhaps merely indifference toward, the current government of Cuba. None of these bombings had caused deaths or mutilations, although bombings which did had become commonplace enough in Miami during the 1970s to create a market for devices designed to flick the ignition in a parked car by remote signal, enabling the intended victim to watch what might have been his own incineration from across the street, an interested bystander.

Many of the bombings mentioned in the government's case against Eduardo Arocena involved what the FBI called his signature, a pocket-watch timer with a floral backpiece. All had been claimed, in communiqués to local Spanish radio stations and newspapers, by Omega 7, which was by the time of these Arocena trials perhaps the most extensively prosecuted and so the most widely known of all the exile action groups operating out of Miami and New Jersey, where there had been since the beginning of the exile a small but significant exile concentration. Omega 7, the leader of which used the code name "Omar," was said by the FBI to have been involved in not only the machine-gunning in Queens of Félix García Rodríguez and the attempted car-bombing in Manhattan of Raúl Roa Kouri (whose driver had discovered the bag of plastique under the car, which was parked at 12 East Eighty-first Street) but also in the 1979 murder in Union City, New Jersey, of Eulalio José Negrin, an exile who supported the normalization of relations between the United States and Cuba and so was killed by a fusillade of semiautomatic fire as he got into a car with his thirteen-year-old son.

Omega 7 had claimed, in New York, the 1979 TWA terminal bombing at Kennedy airport. Omega 7 had claimed the 1978 Avery Fisher Hall bombing at Lincoln Center. Omega 7 had claimed, in Manhattan alone, the 1975 and 1977 bombings of the Venezuelan Mission to the United Nations on East Fifty-first Street, the 1976 and 1978 bombings at the Cuban Mission to the United Nations on East Sixty-seventh Street, the two 1979 bombings of the relocated Cuban Mission to the United Nations on Lexington Avenue, the 1979 bombing of the Soviet Mission to the United Nations on East Sixty-seventh Street, the 1978 bombing of the office of *El Diario–La Prensa* on Hudson Street, the 1980 bombing of the Soviet Union's Aeroflot ticket office on Fifth Avenue, and, by way of protesting the inclusion of Cuban boxers on the card at Madison Square Garden, the 1978 bombing of the adjacent Gerry Cosby Sporting Goods store at 2 Penn Plaza.

The issue in dispute, then, during the three trials that made up *United States of America* v. *Eduardo Arocena*, the first in New York and the second and third in Miami, was not whether Omega 7 had committed the acts mentioned in the indictments, but whether Eduardo Arocena was in fact its leader, "Omar." The government continued to maintain, with considerable success, that he was. Eduardo Arocena continued to maintain that he was not, notwithstanding the fact that he had in 1982 talked at some length to the FBI, in a room at the Ramada Inn near the Miami airport, about Omega 7 actions; had declared during his New York trial that he "unconditionally supported" those actions; and had advised the second of his Miami juries that they had in him "the most confirmed terrorist of all," one who would never repent. "*Padre*, forgive them," Eduardo Arocena had said when this jury handed down its verdicts of guilty on all counts. "For they know not what they do." Miriam Arocena, a small intense woman who strained forward in her seat during testimony and moved to crouch protectively behind her husband whenever the lawyers were conferring with the judge, had called the trial a "comedy," "a farce the government of the United States is carrying out in order to benefit Fidel Castro."

Early in the course of this third Arocena trial I had spent some time at the federal courthouse in downtown Miami, watching the federal prosecutors enter their physical evidence, the wigs and the hairpieces and the glue and the Samsonite attaché cases ("Contents—one pair black gloves, one cheesecloth Handi Wipe rag," or "Contents—one .38-caliber revolver") seized at the bungalow on Southwest Seventh Street in which Eduardo Arocena had been apprehended: an entire modus operandi for the hypothetical Omar, conjured up from the brassbound trunks which the prosecution hauled into court every morning. There was the Browning 9mm pistol. There was the sales receipt for the Browning, as well as for the .25-caliber

Beretta Jetfire, the AR-15, and the UZI. There were
the timers and there were the firecracker fuses. There
were the Eveready Energizer alkaline batteries. There
was the target list, with the names and the locations of
offending businesses, some of them underscored: *Réplica* magazine, Padron Cigars, Almacén El Español,
Ebenezer Trading Agency, a half dozen others. All
that was missing finally was the explosive material itself, the stuff, the dynamite or the plastique, but the
defendant, according to the government, had already
advised the FBI that the military plastique called C-4
could be readily obtained on the street in Miami.

This was all engrossing, not least because it was curiously artless, devoid of much instinct for the clandestine, the wigs and the hairpieces notwithstanding.
The sales receipts for the Browning and for the Beretta
and for the AR-15 and for the UZI were in the defendant's own name. The target list bore on its upper-
left-hand corner the notation TARGETS, suggesting an
indifference to discovery which tended to undermine
the government's exhaustive cataloging of that which
had been discovered. A man who buys a Browning
and a Beretta and an AR-15 and an UZI under his
own name does not have as his first interest the successful evasion of American justice. A man who com-
piles a target list under the heading TARGETS may in
fact have a first interest best served by disclosure, the
inclination toward public statement natural to someone who sees himself as engaged not in a crime but a
crusade. HEROES DE OMEGA 7, as the Omega 7 stencils

were lettered. The stencils were Exhibit 3036, recovered by the FBI from a self-storage locker on Southwest Seventy-second Street. LA VERDAD ES NUESTROS.

There was flickering all through this presentation of the government's evidence a certain stubborn irritability, a sense of crossed purposes, crossed wires, of cultures not exactly colliding but glancing off one another, at unpromising angles. Eduardo Arocena's attorney, a rather rumpled Cuban who had adopted as his general strategy the argument that this trial was taking place at all only because the United States had caved in to what he called "the international community," looked on with genial contempt. The government attorneys, young and well-pressed, rummaged doggedly through their trunks, property masters for what had become in Miami, after some years of trials in which the defense talked about the international community and the prosecution about cheesecloth Handi Wipe rags, a kind of local puppet theater, to which the audience continued to respond in ways novel to those unfamiliar with the form.

This was a theater in which the defendant was always cast as the hero and martyr, not at all because the audience believed him wrongly accused, innocent of whatever charges had been trumped up against him, but precisely because the audience believed him to be guilty. The applause, in other words, was for the action, not for the actor. "Anybody who fights communism has my sympathy," the head of the 2506 Brigade told the *Miami Herald* at the time of Eduardo Arocena's arrest. "The best communist is a dead communist. If that is his way to fight, I won't condemn him." Andres Nazario Sargen of Alpha 66 had said this: "He is a person who chose that path for the liberation of Cuba. We have to respect his position but we think our methods are more effective."

Nor was this response confined exclusively to those members of the audience who, like the men of the 2506 or Alpha 66, might be expected to exhibit a certain institutional tolerance toward bombing as a political tactic. "It's like asking the Palestinian people about Arafat," the news director of WQBA, the Miami radio station that calls itself *La Cubanísima*, had said to the *Herald* about Eduardo Arocena. "He may be a terrorist, but to the Palestinian people he's not thought of that way." All *el exilio* stood by its men of action. When, for example, after Eduardo Arocena's arrest in July of 1983, a fund for his defense was organized within the exile community, one of the contributors was Xavier Suarez, who was that year running a losing campaign for the post to which he was later elected, mayor of Miami. Xavier Suarez was brought to this country as a child, in 1960. He is a graduate of Villanova. He is a graduate of Harvard Law. He has a master's degree in public policy from the John F. Kennedy School of Government at Harvard. He said about Eduardo Arocena that he preferred to think of him not as a terrorist, but a freedom fighter.

Sometimes (when, say, Xavier Suarez says that he prefers to think of Eduardo Arocena not as a terrorist but a freedom fighter, or when, say, Xavier Suarez stands on the back of a Mazda pickup and speaks of the right to be on the other side of the street as unfortunate) words are believed in Miami to be without consequence. Other times they are not. Among the bombs which Omega 7 was credited with having left around Miami in January of 1983, a period of considerable industry for Omega 7, was one at the office of *Réplica*, a Spanish-language weekly largely devoted to soft news and entertainment gossip (CATHY LEE CROSBY: EL SEXO ES MUY IMPORTANTE PARA ELLA is a not atypical photo caption) and edited by an exile named Max Lesnik. Max Lesnik was, in the period after Fidel Castro's 1953 attack on the Moncada Barracks, a youth leader in the Cuban People's Party, the party founded by Eduardo Chibás and known as the "Ortodoxo" party. Opposed to Batista, Max Lesnik was also opposed to Castro, on the grounds that he and his 26 Julio were destructive to the anti-Batista movement. During the time Castro was in the Sierra Maestra, Max Lesnik was working underground in Havana against Batista, not with the 26 Julio but with the Segundo Frente del Escambray, and it was he, in the waning days of 1958, who interested the CIA in the last-ditch attempt to bring Carlos Prío back from Miami as Batista's successor. He made his final break with Castro, and with Cuba, in 1961.

This demonstrable lack of enthusiasm for Fidel Castro notwithstanding, Max Lesnik was considered, by some people in Miami, insufficiently anti-Castro, principally because he, or *Réplica*, had a history of using what were seen to be the wrong words. "Negotiation," for example, was a wrong word, and so, in this context, was "political," as in "a political approach." A political approach implied give-and-take, even compromise, an unthinkable construct in a community organized exclusively around the principle of implacable resistance, and it was the occasional discussion of such an approach in the pages of *Réplica* that had caused *Réplica* to be underscored on Eduardo Arocena's target list, and five bombs to have been left at the *Réplica* office between 1981 and 1984.

Some of *Réplica*'s trouble on this point dated from 1974, when a contributor named Luciano Nieves suggested that the way to bring Fidel Castro down might be "politically," by working with Cubans within Cuba in an effort to force elections and the acceptance of a legal opposition. Someone who did not agree with Luciano Nieves broke a chair over his head in the Versailles, a Cuban restaurant on Southwest Eighth Street where many of the more visible figures in *el exilio* turn up late in the evening. Several other people who did not agree with Luciano Nieves conspired to try, in November of 1974, to assassinate him, a count on which three members of an action group called the Pragmatistas were later tried and convicted, but Luciano Nieves, and *Réplica*, persisted.

In February of 1975, two days after *Réplica* published his declaration that he would return to Cuba to participate in any election Fidel Castro should call, Luciano Nieves was shot and killed, in the parking lot of Variety Children's Hospital in Miami, an event construed locally as his own fault. "I'm glad I never finally came out publicly in favor of peaceful coexistence with Castro," an unidentified professor at what was then Miami-Dade Junior College was quoted as having said a few days later in the *Miami News*, in a story headlined INTELLECTUALS FEARFUL AFTER CUBAN KILLING. "Now, I'll be more than careful not to. Cubans are apparently very sensitive to that." The incident in the parking lot of Variety Children's Hospital was mentioned to me by a number of people during the time I spent in Miami, always to this corrective point.

10

THE bomb Eduardo Arocena was believed to have left at the *Réplica* office in January of 1983 did not, as it happened, go off, but another bomb credited that month to Omega 7 did, this one at a factory on Flagler Street owned by an exiled cigar manufacturer named Orlando Padron. Orlando Padron's treason, as it was viewed by many, had been to visit Havana in 1978 (he was said to have been photographed handing Fidel Castro a Padron cigar) as a member of the "Committee of 75," a participant in what was called the *diálogo*, or dialogue, a word with the same reverberations as "political."

The *diálogo* began as an essay into private diplomacy on the part of a prominent exile banker, Bernardo Benes, whose somewhat visionary notion it was that the exiles themselves, with the tacit cooperation of the Carter administration, could, in what was to become a series of visits to Havana, open a continuing discussion with the Cuban government. Secretary of State Cyrus Vance was approached. The National Security Council and the CIA and the FBI were consulted. The visits to Havana took place, and resulted in two concessions, one an agreement by the Cuban government to release certain political prisoners, some thirty-six hundred in all, the other an agreement allowing exiles who wished to visit relatives in Cuba to do so on seven-day package tours.

Such agreements might have seemed, outside Miami, unexceptionable. Such agreements might even have seemed, outside Miami, to serve the interests of the exile community, but to think this would be to miss the drift of the exile style. Americans, it is often said in Miami, will act always in their own interests, an indictment. Miami Cubans, by implicit contrast, take their stand on a higher ground, *la lucha* as a sacred abstraction, and any talk about "interests," or for that matter "agreements," remains alien to the local temperament, which is absolutist, and sacrificial, on the Spanish model.

Which is to say on the Cuban model. ". . . I feel my belief in sacrifice and struggle getting stronger," Fidel Castro wrote from his prison cell on the Isle of Pines on December 19, 1953. "I despise the kind of existence that clings to the miserly trifles of comfort and self-interest. I think that a man should not live beyond the age when he begins to deteriorate, when the flame that lighted the brightest moment of his life has weakened . . ." In exile as well as in situ, this is the preferred Cuban self-perception, the same idealization of gesture and intention which led, in the months and years after the *diálogo*, to bombings and assassinations and to public occasions of excoriation and recantation, to accusations and humiliations which broke some and estranged many; an unloosing of fratricidal furies from which *el exilio* did not entirely recover.

•

Bernardo Benes, the architect of the *diálogo* and its principal surviving victim, arrived at the Miami airport, alone, on November 11, 1960, a day he recalls as the bleakest of his life. He recalls believing that the exile would last at most nine months. He recalls himself as unprepared in every way to accept the exile as an immigration, and yet, like many of the early exiles, a significant number of whom had been educated to move in the necessarily international commercial life of prerevolutionary Havana, Bernardo Benes apparently managed to maintain the notion of Florida as a kind of colonial opportunity, an India to be tapped, and in this spirit he prospered, first as an officer of a Miami savings and loan, Washington Federal, and then as a local entrepreneur. He was, for example, the first exile to own a major automobile dealership in Miami. He was among the first exiles to start a bank in Miami, the Continental. He was also, and this continued to be, in the culturally resistant world of *el exilio*, a more ambiguous distinction, the first exile to travel what has been in provincial American cities a traditional road to assimilation, the visible doing of approved works, the act of making oneself available for this steering committee, for that kickoff dinner.

"I am frank," Bernardo Benes said when I talked to him one morning at his house on Biscayne Bay. "I do not beat around the bush. Until 1977, 1978, I was The Cuban in Miami. This goes back to when I was still at Washington Federal, I was chief of all the branches, I was the contact for Latin America. So sometimes I was working twenty hours a day to make the time, but believe me, I did. There was nothing important happening in Miami that I wasn't involved with. I was the guerrilla in the establishment, the first person to bring other Cubans into the picture." Bernardo Benes paused. "I and I and I and I," he said finally. "And then came the big change in my life. I was no longer the first token Cuban in Miami. I was the Capitán Dreyfus of Miami."

We were sitting at the kitchen counter, drinking the caffeine and sugar infusion that is Cuban coffee, and as Bernardo Benes began to talk about the *diálogo* and its aftermath he glanced repeatedly at his wife, a strikingly attractive woman who was clearing the breakfast dishes with the brisk, definite movements of someone who has only a limited enthusiasm for the discussion at hand. The *diálogo*, Bernardo Benes said, had come about by "pure chance." There had been, he said, a family vacation in Panama. There had been in Panama, he said, a telephone call from a friend, an entreaty to have lunch with two officers of the Cuban government. This lunch in Panama, he said, had been "the beginning of the end."

There was about this account a certain foretold quality, a collapsing of sequence, as in a dream, or an accident report taken from the sole survivor. Somewhere after the beginning there had been the meetings in Washington with Cyrus Vance and the involvement of the FBI and the CIA and the National Security Council. Somewhere before the end there had been the meetings in Havana with Fidel Castro, 14 meetings, 120 hours during which the first exile to own a major automobile dealership in Miami talked one on one with the number one most hated man in Miami.

The end itself, what Bernardo Benes called the castigation, the casting out, had of course been in Miami, and it had begun, as many such scourgings have begun in Miami, with the long invective exhortations of those Spanish-language radio stations on which *el exilio* depends not only for news but for the daily dissemination of rumor and denunciation. Bernardo Benes was said on the radio to be a communist. Bernardo Benes was said to be a Castro agent. Bernardo Benes was said to be at best a *tonto útil*, or *idiota útil*, a useful fool, which is what exiles call one another when they wish to step back from the precipice of the legally actionable.

"This is Miami," Bernardo Benes said about the radio attacks. "Pure Miami. A million Cubans are blackmailed, totally controlled, by three radio stations. I feel sorry for the Cuban community in Miami. Because they have imposed on themselves, by way of the Right, the same condition that Castro has imposed on Cuba. Total intolerance. And ours is worse. Because it is entirely voluntary."

Bernardo Benes again glanced at his wife, who stood now against the kitchen sink, her arms folded. "My bank was picketed for three weeks." He shrugged. "Every morning when I walked in, twenty or thirty people would be screaming whatever they could think to call me. Carrying signs. Telling people to close their accounts. If I went to a restaurant with my wife, people would come to the table and call me names. But maybe the worst was something I learned only a few months ago. My children never told me at the time, my wife never told me, they knew what I was going through. Here is what I just learned: my children's friends were never allowed to come to our house. Because their parents were afraid. All the parents were afraid their children might be at our house when the bomb went off."

This would not have been a frivolous fear. The *diálogo* took place in the fall of 1978. In April of 1979 a twenty-six-year-old participant in the *diálogo* named Carlos Muñiz Varela was murdered in San Juan, Puerto Rico, by a group calling itself "Comando Cero." In November of 1979 there was the murder in Union City of another participant in the *diálogo*, Eulalio José Negrin, the one who was stepping into his car with his son when two men in ski masks appeared and the fusillade started. The October 1978 bombing at *El Diario-La Prensa* in New York was connected to the *diálogo:* the newspaper had run an editorial in favor of the arrangement allowing exiles to visit Cuba. The March 1979 bombing at Kennedy airport (the bomb was in a suitcase about to be loaded into the hold of an L-1011, TWA #17, due to leave for Los Angeles twelve minutes later with more than 150 people already aboard) was connected to the *diálogo:* TWA had provided equipment for some charters to Cuba.

The scars *el exilio* inflicts upon its own do not entirely heal, nor are they meant to. Seven years after the *diálogo*, when Bernardo Benes's daughter was shopping at Burdines and presented her father's credit card, the saleswoman, a Cuban, looked at the name, handed back the card, and walked away. Bernardo Benes himself sold his business interests, and is no longer so visible a presence around Miami. "You move on," he said. "For example something has happened in my life at age fifty. I have become hedonistic. I lost twenty-five pounds, I joined a sauna, and in my garage you will find a new convertible. Which I drive around Miami. With the top down."

Bernardo Benes and I spoke, that morning in the pleasant house on Biscayne Bay, for an hour or so. From the windows of that house it was possible to look across the bay at the Miami skyline, at buildings through which Bernardo Benes had moved as someone entitled. Mrs. Benes spoke only once, to interrupt her husband with a protective burst of vehement Spanish. "No Cubans will read what she writes," Bernardo Benes said in English. "You will be surprised," his wife said in English. "Anything I say can be printed, that's the price of being married to me, I'm a tough cookie," Bernardo Benes said in English. "All right," his wife said, in English, and she walked away. "You just make your life insurance more."

11

SOME exiles in Miami will now allow that Bernardo Benes was perhaps a sacrificial victim, the available if accidental symbol of a polarization within the exile which had actually begun some years before, and had brought into question the very molecular code of the community, its opposition to Fidel Castro. There were at the time of the *diálogo*, and are still, certain exiles, most of them brought to the United States as children, fewer of them living now in Miami than in New York and Washington, who were not in fact opposed to Fidel Castro. Neither were many of them exactly pro-Castro, except to the extent that they believed that there was still in progress in Cuba a revolutionary process, and that this process, under the direction of Fidel Castro or not under the direction of Fidel Castro, should continue. *Somos Cubanos*, the editors of *Areíto*, published as a quarterly by the Círculo de Cultura Cubana in New York, had declared in their first issue, in April 1974. "While recognizing that the revolutionary process has implied sacrifices, sufferings and errors," the *Areíto* manifesto had continued, "we maintain that Cuba in 1958 needed measures capable of radically transforming its political, social and economic structures. We understand that that process has established the basis for a more just and egalitarian society, and that it has irreversibly taken root in Cuban society."

The editors of *Areíto* had put the name of the Havana poet Roberto Fernández Retamar on their masthead, and also that of Gabriel García Márquez. In 1984, for the tenth anniversary issue, they had reprinted the 1974 manifesto, and added: "Solidarity with the Cuban revolution was and is a position based on principle for our Editorial Board. . . . The ten years that have passed took us on a return trip to Cuba, to confront for ourselves in its entirety the complexity of that society, and by that token, to rid ourselves of the romantic notions which were typical of our group at that time. . . . Because of that, today we assume our position with more firmness and awareness of its consequences." *Areíto* contributors thought of themselves less as exiles than as "Cubans outside Cuba," and of exile Miami, in the words of this tenth anniversary issue, as "the deformed foetus of Meyer Lansky, the Cuban lumpen bourgeoisie and the North American security state."

The *Grupo Areíto*, as *Areíto*'s editors and contributors came to call themselves, had perhaps never represented more than a very small number of exiles, but these few were young, articulate, and determined to be heard. There had been members of the *Areíto* group involved in the Washington lobby originally called the Cuban-American Committee for the Normalization of Relations with Cuba, not to be confused with its polar opposite, the Cuban American National

Foundation. There had been members of the *Areíto* group involved with Bernardo Benes in those visits to Cuba which constituted the *diálogo*. (Carlos Muñiz Varela, the member of the Committee of 75 who had been assassinated in 1979 in San Juan, Puerto Rico, was a founder of *Areíto*.) There had been members of the *Areíto* group involved in the inception of the Antonio Maceo Brigade, which was organized along the lines of the largely Anglo Venceremos Brigade and offered working sojourns in Cuba to, in the words of its 1978 statement of purpose, "any young Cuban who (1) left Cuba by family decision, (2) has not participated in counterrevolutionary activities and would not support violence against the revolution, and (3) defines him or herself as opposed to the blockade and in favor of the normalization of relations between the United States and Cuba."

These children of *el exilio* who had taken to talking about the deformed foetus of the North American security state and to writing articles with such titles as "Introduction to the Sandinista Documentary Cinema" were not, in other words, pursuing a course which was likely to slip the attention of exile Miami, nor did it. There were bombings. There were death threats. Members of the Antonio Maceo Brigade were referred to as *traidores*, traitors, and the brigade itself as a demonic strategy by which Fidel Castro hoped to divide the exile along generational lines. *Areíto* was said in Miami to be directly funded by the Cuban government, a charge its editors dismissed as a slander, in fact a *cantinela*, the kind of repeated refrain that set the teeth on edge. "It's very difficult for people like us, who maintain a position like we do, to live in Miami," an *Areíto* board member named Marifeli Pérez-Stable told the *Miami Herald* in 1983, by way of explaining why she lived in New York. "Everybody knows everything, and it makes it difficult for those who are fingered as having a pro-Castro position to do something as simple as going to the market."

Marifeli Pérez-Stable was in 1983, when she spoke to the *Herald*, thirty-four. Lourdes Casal, a founder of *Areíto* and for many people its personification, was in 1981, when she died in Havana, forty-two. *Areíto* was published not at all during 1985 or 1986. Time passes and heat goes, although less reliably in Miami, where, at the "First Annual Festival of Hispanic Theatre" in May of 1986, all scheduled performances of a one-act play by a New York playwright and former *Areíto* contributor named Dolores Prida were, after several days of radio alarms and a bomb threat, canceled.

The play itself, *Coser y Cantar*, described by the *Herald* theater reviewer as "pleasant if flawed," a "modest piece" about an Hispanic woman living in New York and her Anglo alter ego (the latter wants to make lists and march at the United Nations, the former to read *Vanidades* and shop for sausage at Casa Moneo), seemed not to be the question here. The question seemed to be Dolores Prida's past, which included connections with *Areíto* and with the *diálogo* and with the Cuban-American Committee, three strikes against her in a city where even one proved allegiance to what was referred to locally as "the so-called Cuban 'revolution.' " Dolores Prida was said by the news director of WQBA-*La Cubanísima* to be "an enemy of the exiles." That Dolores Prida should even think of visiting Miami was said by Metro-Dade commissioner George Valdes to be "a Castroite and communist plan . . . a tactic of the Cuban government to divide us and make us look bad."

Nonetheless, at the height of her local celebrity, Dolores Prida did visit Miami, where, as part of a conference at Miami-Dade Community College on "The Future of Hispanic Theatre in Miami: Goals and Constraints," she supervised a previously unscheduled reading of *Coser y Cantar*, the audience for which had been frisked by Miami police with handheld metal detectors. Dolores Prida told the *Herald* that the word "communist" was used so loosely in Miami that she did not know what it meant. "If you're progressive," Dolores Prida said, "you're a communist." Dolores Prida told the *Herald* that the only card she carried was American Express. Dolores Prida, who was at the time of this dispute forty-three years old, also told the *Herald* that the only city other than Miami in which she had ever been afraid to express herself, the only other place "where people look over their shoulder to see if they can say what they were going to say," was Havana.

In many ways these midlife survivors of what had been a student movement seem familiar to us. We have met, if not them, their American-born counterparts, people who at one time thought and in many cases still think along lines they might or might not call, as the *Areíto* group often called itself, "progressive." These were exiles who, to at least some extent, thought of America's interests as their own, and of America's issues as their own; who seemed to fall, in a way that Miami exiles often did not, within the American experience. They experienced for example the Vietnam War, and the movement against it, as their own, in a way that many Miami exiles, some of whom told me that they had avoided the draft not because they opposed the war but because they had been at the time engaged in a war which meant more to them, did not. They experienced the social changes of the sixties and seventies in a way that many Miami exiles did not, and they had been in some cases confused and torn by those changes, which seemed to be, in a light way, part of what Dolores Prida's play was about.

In other words they were Americans, yet they were not. *Somos Cubanos.* They remained Cubans, and they remained outside Cuba, and as Cubans outside Cuba but estranged from *el exilio* they came to occupy a particularly hermetic vacuum, one in which, as in *el exilio* itself, positions were defined and redefined and schisms were divined and dissected and a great deal of what went on floated somewhere in a diaspora of its own. I recall a 1984 issue of *Areíto* in which several pages were given over to the analysis of a schism between the *Areíto* group and the generally like-minded Institute of Cuban Studies, and of what ideological error had caused the Institute of Cuban Studies not only to suggest that the late Lourdes Casal had "deviated from the canons of socialist realism" but to misrepresent her position on the relationship between the intellectual and the Cuban revolutionary process, a position made clear for example in her later refinement of her original 1972 statement on the case of the poet Heberto Padilla. These were questions which seemed at a significant tonal remove from those then being asked in New York or New Haven or Boston or Berkeley, although not, curiously enough, from those then being asked in Miami.

On January 9, 1961, at a time when the Cuban revolution was two years under way and the 2506 Brigade was training in Guatemala for the April invasion, the United States Department of State granted to a Miami priest, Monsignor Bryan O. Walsh, the authority to grant a visa waiver to any Cuban child between the ages of six and sixteen who wished to enter the United States under the guardianship of the Catholic diocese of Miami. According to *Catholicism in South Florida: 1868–1968*, by Michael J. McNally, a Miami priest and professor of church history at St. Vincent de Paul Seminary in Boynton Beach, such waivers were issued, between January of 1961 and September of 1963, to 14,156 children, each of whom was sent alone, by parents or guardians still living in Cuba, to live in special camps established and operated by the Unaccompanied Children's Program of the Diocese of Miami.

There were, in all, six such camps, the last of which did not close until the middle of 1981. The reason that these camps were established and the Unaccompanied Children's Program was initiated, Father McNally tells us, was that, by the end of 1960, "rumors were rife" that Fidel Castro planned to send Cuban children to work on Soviet farms, and that, during 1961, "rumors spread" that Fidel Castro had still another plan, "to have children ages three to ten live in state-run dormitories, seeing their parents for only two days a month." It was "to avoid these two possibilities" that parents dispatched their children to Miami and the Unaccompanied Children's Program, which was also known, according to Father McNally, as "Operation Pedro Pan."

No spread rumor goes unrewarded. In *Contra Viento y Marea*, edited by Lourdes Casal and published in 1978 by Casa de las Américas in Havana, there appear a number of descriptions, under the joint byline *Grupo Areíto*, of camp life as it was experienced by those who lived it. These members of the *Areíto* group who arrived in the United States as wards of Operation Pedro Pan characterized this experience, in *Contra Viento y Marea*, as "perhaps the most enduring" of their lives. They described the camps as the "prehistory" of their radicalization, the places in which they first formulated, however inchoately, the only analysis which seemed to them to explain the "lunacy," the "political troglodytism," the "traumatic experience," of having been banished by their parents to live in a barracks in a foreign country. The speakers in this part of *Contra Viento y Marea* are both those who spent time in the camps as children and those who worked in them as adults:

> It was said that Monsignor Walsh . . . had practically unlimited authority to issue visa waivers to children in order to "save them from communism." This episode in our recent history can be seen in retrospect as a period of near-delirium, based as it was on the insistent propaganda that the revolutionary government would strip parents of their authority and send their children to Russia. . . .

> The first time I began to see through and re-evaluate a few things was when I was working at Opa-Locka, one of the camps where they brought the children who came alone from Cuba. Opa-Locka was managed by the Jesuits. Again and again I asked myself what had motivated these parents to send their children alone to the United States. . . .

> Sometimes we would give little talks to the American Legion Auxiliary ladies, who were fascinated to see these white Cubans who knew how to eat with knives and forks . . . but most of all they wanted to hear the horrible story of how and why we were there: the incredible and sad tale of how communism, in order to destroy parental authority, had been going to put us on boats

bound for Russia. . . . We would sing Cuban songs and the old ladies would go home crying.

It must be said that the Americans were using the Cubans: the mass emigration, the children who came alone . . . The departure of the children was used largely as a propaganda ploy. What came out of the camps would be a wounded generation. . . .

These accounts, however colored, are suggestive. The parents in Cuba had been, as the children put it together, the victims of *una estafa*, a trick, a deceit, since the distinction between being banished to camps in the USSR and banished to camps in the United States lacked, for the children, significance. The nuns in the camps, who had advised their charges that one day they would appreciate this distinction, were, as the children saw it, equally the victims of *una estafa*. The children themselves, some of whom had later become these Cubans outside Cuba but estranged from *el exilio*, these middle-aged scholars and writers whose visits to Miami necessitated metal detectors, had been, as they saw it then and saw it still, "used" by the government of the United States, "utilized" by the government of the United States, "manipulated" by the government of the United States, made by the government of the United States the victims of a "propaganda ploy"; a way of talking about the government of the United States, as it happened, indistinguishable from what was said every day in exile Miami.

12

"THE Miami exiles are not anti-communist," an exile named Carlos M. Luis said one night at dinner. It was about eleven o'clock, the preferred hour for dinner in those exile houses where Spanish manners still prevailed, and there were at the table nine people, eight Cubans and me. There had been before Carlos Luis spoke a good deal of spirited argument. There had been a mounting rhythm of declamation and interruption. Now there was a silence. "The Miami exiles are not anti-communist," Carlos Luis repeated. "I believe this. Anti-communism is not their motivation."

Carlos Luis was the director of the Museo Cubano de Arte y Cultura in Miami, an interesting and complicated man who had entered exile with his wife in 1962, deciding to move to New York after the cultural restructuring which began in Cuba with the confiscation of Orlando Jiménez Leal's documentary film *P.M.*, or *Pasado Meridiano*, and led eventually to Fidel Castro's declaration that there was no art, or would be no art, outside the revolution. "The *P.M.* affair," as it was called in Miami, had plunged Havana into a spiral of confrontation and flagellation not unlike that which later characterized *el exilio*, and was for many a kind of turning point.

It was the *P.M.* affair, involving as it did the banning of a film showing "decadent" nightlife in Havana, which more or less codified such repressive moves as the official persecution of homosexuals later examined by Orlando Jiménez Leal and the Academy Award–winning cinematographer Nestor Almendros, by then both in exile, in *Mauvaise Conduite*. It was the *P.M.* affair which had in fact gotten Nestor Almendros, at the time a young filmmaker who had written admiringly about *P.M.*, fired from his job at *Bohemia*, the Havana weekly which had by then closed itself down and been restaffed by people closer to the direction in which the regime seemed to be moving. And it was the *P.M.* affair which had caused a number of Cuban artists and intellectuals to doubt that there would be room within this revolution for whatever it was that they might have valued above the revolution; to conclude that, as Carlos Luis put it, "it was time to leave, there was no more for me in staying."

"The first group left because they were Batistianos," Carlos Luis said now, reaching for a bottle of wine. "The second group left because they were losing their property." Carlos Luis paused, and poured an inch of wine into his glass. "Then," he said, "the people started coming who were unhappy because they couldn't get toothpaste."

"You mean these exiles were anti-Castro but not necessarily anti-communist," our host, an exile, said, as if to clarify the point not for himself but for me.

"Anti-Castro, yes," Carlos Luis had shrugged. "Anti-Castro it goes without saying."

That the wish to see Fidel Castro removed from power in Cuba did not in itself constitute a political philosophy was a point rather more appreciated in *el exilio*, which had as its legacy a tradition of considerable political sophistication, than in Washington, which tended to accept the issue as an idea, and so to see Cuban exiles as refugees not just from Castro but from politics. In fact exile life in Miami was dense with political distinctions, none of them exactly in the American grain. Miami was for example the only American city I had ever visited in which it was not unusual to hear one citizen describe the position of another as "Falangist," or as "essentially Nasserite." There were in Miami exiles who defined themselves as communists, anti-Castro. There were in Miami a significant number of exile socialists, also anti-Castro, but agreed on only this single issue. There were in Miami two prominent groups of exile anarchists, many still in their twenties, all anti-Castro, and divided from one another, I was told, by "personality differences," "personality differences" being the explanation Cubans tend to offer for anything from a dinner-table argument to a coup.

This urge toward the staking out of increasingly recondite positions, traditional to exile life in Europe and in Latin America, remained, in South Florida, exotic, a nervous urban brilliance not entirely apprehended by local Anglos, who continued to think of exiles as occupying a fixed place on the political spectrum, one usually described as "right-wing," or "ultra-conservative." It was true enough that there were a number of exiles in Miami who believed the most effective extant political leaders in the hemisphere (aside from Fidel Castro, to whom diabolic powers were attributed) to be General Augusto Pinochet of Chile and General Alfredo Stroessner of Paraguay. In fact those two names were heard with some frequency even in the conversation of exiles who did not share this belief, usually turning up in the "as" construction, in which the speaker thinks to disarm the listener by declaring himself "every bit as hostile to the Pinochet government," or "just as unalterably opposed to General Stroessner," as to Fidel Castro. It was also true enough that there were a number of Cubans in Miami, most notably those tobacco growers who between the fall of Fulgencio Batista and the fall of Anastasio Somoza had managed to maintain their operations in Nicaragua, who supported the military leadership of the Nicaraguan contras not in spite of but precisely because of whatever association that leadership had with the Somoza militia.

Still, "right-wing," on the American spectrum, where political positions were understood as marginally different approaches to what was seen as a shared goal, seemed not to apply. This was something different, a view of politics as so central to the human condition that there may be no applicable words in the political vocabulary of most Americans. Virtually every sentient member of the Miami exile community was on any given day engaged in what was called an "ideological confrontation" with some other member of the Miami exile community, over points which were passionately debated at meals and on the radio and in the *periodiquitos*, the throwaway newspapers which appeared every week on Southwest Eighth Street. Everything was read. I was asked one day by several different people if I had seen a certain piece that morning, by a writer whose name I did not recognize. The piece, it turned out, had appeared not in the *Miami Herald* or the *Miami News*, not in *El Herald* or *Diario Las Americas*, not in any of the *periodiquitos* and not even in *The New York Times*, but in *El Tiempo*, one day late from Bogotá. Analysis was close, and overcharged. Obscure points were "clarified," and immediately "answered." The whole of exile Miami could engage itself in the morning deconstruction of, say, something said by Roberto Fernández Retamar in Havana as reported by *El País* in Madrid and "answered" on the radio in Miami.

I talked one evening to Agustin Tamargo, an exile whose radio broadcasts with such prominent exiles as the novelist Guillermo Cabrera Infante and the poet Heberto Padilla and the legendary 26 Julio *comandante* Huber Matos, what Agustin Tamargo called "all the revolutionary people," had tended over the years to attract whatever excess animus happened to be loose in the community. "I come from a different place on the political spectrum than most of the other radio commentators here," Agustin Tamargo said. "There are many Batista people in Miami. They call me a communist because I wrote in *Bohemia*, which was to them a leftist-Marxist paper. Actually it was maybe center."

Agustin Tamargo entered exile in 1960, the year *Bohemia*, which had been perhaps the most influential voice of the anti-Batista movement, suspended its own publication with the declaration "this is a revolution betrayed." After he left Havana he was managing editor of *Bohemia*-in-exile, which was published first in New York, with what Agustin Tamargo believes to have been CIA money, and then in Caracas, with what he calls "different business partners, completely separated from American interests," the entire question of "American interests" remaining in Miami an enduring preoccupation. I recall one visit when everyone to whom I spoke seemed engaged in either an attack on or a defense of the exiled writer and former political prisoner Carlos Alberto Montaner, who had written a column from Madrid which some found, because it seemed to them to suggest that Fidel Castro could be tolerated to the extent that he could be separated from Soviet interests, insufficiently separated from American interests. I was advised by one exile that "Montaner thinks about Fidel exactly the way Reagan thinks about Fidel," not, since even those exiles who voted in large numbers for Ronald Reagan in 1980 and 1984 did so despite their conviction that he was bent on making a secret deal with Fidel Castro, an endorsement.

There seemed in fact very few weeks in Miami when, on the informal network the community used to talk to itself, one or another exile spokesman was not being excoriated on or defended against this charge of being insufficiently separated from American interests. One week it was said that the poet Jorge Valls, because he had left Cuba after twenty years in prison and suggested on the radio in Miami that there should be "an interchange of ideas" between the United States and Havana, was insufficiently separated from American interests. Another week it was said that Armando Valladares, whose *Contra Toda Esperanza*, an account of the twenty-two years he had spent imprisoned by Fidel Castro, appeared in this country as *Against All Hope*, was, because he had received support from the National Endowment for Democracy, insufficiently separated from American interests. "There's nothing wrong with American money," Agustin Tamargo had said the evening we talked, by way of amending an impassioned indictment of another exile who was, he believed, getting it. "Or Chinese money or any other kind. I will take it if they give it to me. But only to do what I want to do. Not what they want me to do. There is the difference."

In Miami, where he was at the time we met doing a nightly broadcast for WOCN-Union Radio about which there was controversy even within the station itself, Agustin Tamargo was regarded as an eccentric and even a quixotic figure, which seemed to be how he construed his role. "Fifty thousand people listen to me every night," he said. "And every night I say Franco was a killer. Every night I say Pinochet is an assassin. Most of the other Cuban commentators here never say anything about Pinochet. This is a program on which people say every kind of thing about the Cuban past. We say that maybe things before the revolution were not so golden as people here like to think. And still they listen. Which suggests to me that maybe the exile is not so one-sided as the communists say it is."

We were sitting that evening in an office at WOCN-Union Radio on Flagler Street, and outside in the reception room there was an armed security guard who would later walk Agustin Tamargo to his car, Miami being a city in which people who express their opinions on the radio every night tend, particularly since 1976, when a commentator named Emilio Milian got his legs blown off in the WQBA-*La Cubanísima* parking lot, to put a little thought into the walk to the car. "Listen to me," Agustin Tamargo said. "You do see a change here. A few years ago no one in exile would admit that any kind of solution to the Cuban situation could come from inside. They wouldn't hear of it. Now they admit it. They admit that a rebellion inside Cuba could lead to a military solution, a coup." Agustin Tamargo had shrugged. "That's a real advance. A few years ago here, you said that, you got killed. Immediately."

Emilio Milian lost his legs because he suggested in a series of editorials on WQBA-*La Cubanísima* that it was counterproductive for exiles to continue bombing and assassinating one another on the streets of Miami. That this was an exceptionable opinion in an American city in 1976 was hard for some Americans to entirely appreciate, just as it was hard for some Americans, accustomed as they were to the official abhorrence of political violence, to appreciate the extent to which many people in Miami regarded such violence as an inevitable and even a necessary thread in the social fabric. The Miami City Commission in 1982 voted a ten-thousand dollar grant to Alpha 66, which was, however venerable, however fixed an element on the Miami landscape, a serious action group, one of the twenty exile groups believed by the House Select Committee on Assassinations in 1978 to have had "the motivation, capability and resources" to have assassinated President John F. Kennedy, and one of the two, according to the committee's report, about which there were as well "indications of a possible connection with figures named in the Kennedy assassination, specifically with Lee Harvey Oswald." At a 1983 meeting, the same Miami City Commission proclaimed March twenty-fifth "Dr. Orlando Bosch Day," in recognition of the Miami pediatrician who was then imprisoned at Cuartel San Carlos in Caracas on charges of planning the bombing in 1976 of a Cubana DC-8 off Barbados, killing all seventy-three passengers, including twenty-four members of the Cuban national fencing team.

The case of Orlando Bosch was interesting. He had been, before he moved to Miami in July of 1960, the chief of the 26 Julio for Las Villas Province. During his first month in Miami he had helped to launch the insurgent group called the MIRR, the Movimiento Insurreccional de Recuperación Revolucionaria, which became known that August, when four Castro army officers and a hundred of their men deserted their posts and took up arms in the Las Villas mountains. Over the next several years in Miami, Orlando Bosch was arrested repeatedly on charges connected with MIRR activity, but was, until 1968, repeatedly acquitted. In 1968 he was finally convicted on a federal charge, that of shelling a Polish freighter in the Port of Miami, was sentenced to ten years and paroled after four. In 1974, back in Miami and subpoenaed for questioning in the assassination of an exile leader, Orlando Bosch had broken parole by fleeing the country.

There were, in all, four Cuban exiles charged by Venezuela in the 1976 Cubana bombing. Two were accused of actually placing the bomb on the plane and the other two, one of whom was Dr. Bosch and the other of whom was a 2506 member named Luis Posada Carriles, of planning or arranging this placement. Not least because Luis Posada Carriles happened to be a former operations chief of the Venezuelan secret police, DISIP, the Cubana case was a sensitive one for Venezuela, and, after a decade of what appeared to many to be stalling actions, Orlando Bosch was in 1986 acquitted by a Venezuelan judge, who noted that at the time the plane actually fell from the sky "citizen Orlando Bosch was not in the company" of the two men accused of placing the bomb, both of whom were convicted. In the case of the fourth defendant, Luis Posada Carriles, there was no final disposition, since he had the year before escaped from the penitentiary in San Juan de Los Morros (aided, it was reported, by $28,600 in payoffs), some sixty miles southwest of Caracas, and appeared to have next surfaced in the Escalón district of San Salvador, living in a rented house and working on the covert contra supply operation at Ilopango air base under the name "Ramon Medina."

The name "Ramon Medina" began coming up in late 1986, at the time the first details of the contra supply network organized by Lieutenant Colonel Oliver North and Major General Richard V. Secord were becoming known, and there was some speculation that his job at Ilopango had been arranged by Felix Rodriguez, also known as Max Gomez, who in turn had been recommended as an adviser to the Salvadoran armed forces by the office of Vice President George Bush. "We have been asked if Mr. Bush knew or knows Ramon Medina," a spokesman for Vice President George Bush said. "The answer is no. The same answer holds for Ramon Posada or any other names or aliases." Some weeks later, in Miami, an exhibition of Orlando Bosch's paintings was held, some sixty oils, priced at $25 to $500 and listed under such titles as *The Southern Coast of Cuba* and *Nightfall in the Tropics*. Tea sandwiches were served, and wine. The president of the Committee to Free Orlando Bosch pointed out that the paintings had certain common motifs, that doors kept turning up, and roads, and bodies of water; that the painter was "always looking for the way to freedom." (Luis Posada Carriles' oils, of Venezuelan landscapes, had been exhibited in Miami a year before.) Orlando Bosch himself was still in jail in Caracas, waiting for yet another obstacle to be negotiated, the confirmation of his acquittal. He was also still, from the point of view of the United States, a fugitive terrorist, someone who, if he tried to re-enter the United States, faced immediate arrest on his parole violation.

That the governing body of an American city should have declared a "day" in honor of someone with so clouded a history might have in most parts of the United States profoundly disturbed the citizens of that city, but Miami was a community in which, as the *Herald* had pointed out in 1985, a significant percentage of the population continued to see Orlando Bosch as a hero. "You are mistaken when you say that 'many exiles believe that Bosch is a hero,' " a letter to *El Herald* complained on this point. "Not just 'many,' as you say, but ALL Cuban exiles believe Dr. Bosch to be so decent a man, so Rambo-like a hero, that, even supposing there were any truth to the allegations about that communist plane crash many years ago, Dr. Bosch would only have been trying to pay back in kind those enemies of this country who, every day, all over the world, are bombing and killing and maiming innocent citizens, including elderly tourists in their wheelchairs." This note of *machismo* was often struck when people mentioned Orlando Bosch. "Most people talk more than they act," an exile named Cosme Barros told the *Herald* after the acquittal in Caracas. "Bosch has acted more than he has talked." "He is how every man should be," an exile named Norma Garcia told the same reporter. "If we had more men like him, today Cuba would be free."

The case of Orlando Bosch and Luis Posada Carriles and the bombing of the Cubana DC-8 had always been complicated, as most stories in this part of the world turned out to be, by more than just one sensitive connection. There had been, besides the line from Luis Posada Carriles to the Venezuelan secret police, visible lines from both Luis Posada Carriles and Orlando Bosch to the government of the United States. According to a 1977 CIA document obtained by the *Miami Herald*, Luis Posada Carriles, who was later called Ramon Medina, had received CIA demolition and weapons training before the Bay of Pigs, had formally joined the CIA in 1965, had worked briefly in Guatemala and then moved on to Venezuela and DISIP, finally resigning as DISIP operations chief in 1974. Throughout this period, according to the 1977 document quoted by the *Herald*, Luis Posada Carriles had remained on the CIA payroll.

Orlando Bosch himself, according to staff interviews conducted by and to CIA and FBI memos released to the 1978 House Select Committee on Assassinations, had been under contract to the CIA during the early 1960s, running, with Evelio Duque of the Ejército Cubano Anticomunista, a camp in Homestead, the last Florida town before the Keys. Orlando Bosch told the House committee staff members who interviewed him in Cuartel San Carlos that he had soon begun to see this Homestead camp as, in the committee's words, "an exercise in futility." He had begun to suspect that such CIA-sponsored camps were, again in the committee's words, "merely a means of keeping the exiles busy." His CIA contact had, he said, "privately and unofficially" confirmed this suspicion.

This was a peculiar climate in South Florida, and had been so since 1960. Signals seemed to get mixed. Transmissions seemed to jam. Some atmospheric anomaly seemed to create trick mirrors, in which those people (or personnel, or assets) who were to be kept busy (or disposed of) and those people who could be strategically deployed (or used) appeared to be one and the same, their image changing with the light, and the distant agenda, in Washington. Sometimes even those people who were to be kept busy (or strategically deployed) and those people who were running the distant agenda appeared to be one and the same, or so it might have seemed to anyone looking in the mirror when the images spoke. "You have to fight violence with violence," Orlando Bosch was quoted as saying in the *Miami News* in 1978. "At times you cannot avoid hurting innocent people." The same year, 1978, Richard Helms, who had been directing CIA operations from Washington during the time Orlando Bosch was running the camp in Homestead, said this to the House Select Committee on Assassinations: "I would like to point out something since we are so deeply into this. When one government is trying to upset another government and the operation is successful, people get killed."

13

In 1985 and 1986 it was said in exile Miami that the coup, the coup in Cuba, the "solution from inside," the "military solution" Agustin Tamargo had mentioned the night we spoke in his office at WOCN-Union Radio, would take place in three, maybe four years. In 1985 and 1986 it was also said in exile Miami that the coup would not take place. In 1985 and 1986 it was also said in exile Miami that the coup, were the coup allowed to take place, which it would not be, would occur along anti-Soviet lines, and could begin among certain officers from the one Cuban military school to which there had been assigned no Soviet trainers. Still, this coup would never take place. The reason this coup would never take place, it was said by various people to whom I spoke in exile Miami in 1985 and 1986, was because "the United States wants a Cuba it can control," because "a coup would mean a new situation," and because "in the changed situation after the coup they would hate the United States even more than the communists do."

The coup which the United States would never allow to take place had in fact by the 1980s largely supplanted, as an exile plot point, the invasion which the United States had never allowed to take place, and was for the time being, until something more concrete came along (the narrative bones for this something, the projected abandonment of the Nicaraguan contras, were of course already in place), the main story line for what *el exilio* continued to see as its betrayal, its utilization, its manipulation, by the government of the United States. A rather unsettling number of exiles to whom I spoke cited, as evidence of Washington's continuing betrayal, the Omega 7 prosecutions. Others cited the Reagan administration's attempts to deport the so-called "Mariel excludables," those refugees whose criminal records would normally be grounds, under American immigration policy, for deportation or exclusion. Many, including Agustin Tamargo, cited Radio Martí, about which there had been, it seemed, considerable controversy within the exile community. "Radio Martí is a department of the Voice of America," Agustin Tamargo had said the evening we met in his office at WOCN-Union Radio. "Which is a guarantee to me that when the American government makes its deal with Fidel Castro, Radio Martí will say amen."

I had then been in Miami only a short time, and had not before been exposed to this local view of Radio Martí as yet another way in which the government of the United States was deceiving the exile community. I said to Agustin Tamargo that I did not quite understand. I said that I, and I believed many other Americans, including several to whom I had talked in Washington who had been involved with the issue as it passed through Congress, had tended to think of

Radio Martí as something the Miami exile community specifically wanted. I said that I had in fact met Miami exiles, for example Jorge Mas Canosa, who had gone to some lengths to see the Radio Martí legislation enacted.

"Rich people," Agustin Tamargo said.

I allowed that this was possibly true.

"The same rich people who are Republicans. Listen. I hate communists, but I hate some of these exiles more." Agustin Tamargo was on this subject a dog with a bone. "They are why we are here all these years. If a man like Che Guevara were on our side, we would have been back in Cuba long ago. However. Instead of Che Guevara, we have Mas Canosa. I'm sorry. I mention him only because he is one of the richest."

This was one of those leaps to the ad hominem toward which exile conversation seemed ever to tend. I had known that there was within the community a certain resistance to the leadership claims of Jorge Mas Canosa and the other supporters of the Cuban American National Foundation. I had also known that resistance derived in part from the well-publicized conviction of the Cuban American National Foundation, a group somewhat more attuned than the average Miami exile to the pitch at which an American congressman is apt to lose eye contact, that exile aims could best be achieved by working within the American political system; that, in other words, the time had passed for running raids on Cuba and shelling Soviet-bloc ships in the Port of Miami. Still, even ad hominem, even given the fact that Jorge Mas Canosa and the Cuban American National Foundation had been largely responsible for Radio Martí, the point about Radio Martí as proof of American perfidy remained obscure to me, and I had looked for help to another exile who had joined us that evening, a young man named Daniel Morcate.

"I disagree with Agustin strongly on Radio Martí," Daniel Morcate had said, and then, deferentially: "But then the whole exile community is divided. On that question." Daniel Morcate, whose wife Gina was a writer and an assistant to Carlos Luis at the Museo Cubano de Arte y Cultura, had left Cuba at fourteen, in 1971. He had spent four years in Madrid and lived since (except for one year, 1979, when he returned to Madrid to work for Carlos Alberto Montaner) in Miami, where he was, at the time we met, working for WOCN-Union Radio and teaching philosophy at St. Thomas University, an institution founded in Miami by Augustinian brothers formerly affiliated with Villanueva University in Havana. He was among those younger exiles who defined themselves as philosophical anarchists. He had stressed that evening that he was "not a man of action," but that, at certain times and under certain conditions, he supported the idea of action. He was, he had said, "a man of words," and he chose them carefully.

As this might suggest, Daniel Morcate's position on Radio Martí and the Cuban American National Foundation (which was to say, I was beginning to see, his position on working within the American system) was subtle, even tortured. His own concerns about Radio Martí had been sufficient to keep him from accepting one of the Radio Martí jobs which had been passed around Miami as a particularly exotic form of patronage, and he differed from those of his contemporaries who did work in Washington, both for Radio Martí and for the Cuban American National Foundation, on several key points. Despite the fact that he was not, as he had said, a man of action, Daniel Morcate did believe, as the Cuban American National Foundation pointedly did not believe, that now was as good a time as any for running physical actions against the government of Cuba. He also believed that groups running such actions should seek support not only from the United States but from other nations.

Still, given these exceptions and under certain limited conditions, he agreed in principle with such Washington exiles of his generation as Ramon Mestre at Radio Martí and Frank Calzón, who was at that time director of the Cuban American National Foundation, that it was possible for exiles to coexist with and even to influence the government of the United States. "I think that many goals of the United States government are very legitimate," Daniel Morcate said. "Many Cubans do. And so they believe that they can use the United States government without compromising their own ideals. This is what many people in the Cuban American National Foundation believe."

"They believe in publicity," Agustin Tamargo had said, interrupting.

"I happen to think that someone like Frank Calzón

is a deep-rooted nationalist," Daniel Morcate had insisted. "I believe that he thinks he is utilizing the United States government." He had paused, and shrugged. "Of course the United States government thinks the same about him."

Agustin Tamargo had been patient. "Look. Radio Martí is an instrument of American foreign policy." He had ticked off the points on his fingers. "The American government decides that it is going to co-exist with Castro and the next day we will have a long story on Radio Martí about our cooperation with the United States government. We have no say in this. In the Reagan administration more than ever. The Reagan administration has one goal in Cuba. Which is to separate Castro from Moscow. Not to overthrow Castro. They put in jail anybody here who says he wants to overthrow Castro. They put in jail the Omega 7. We have been taught to throw bombs, taught to work with every kind of *desgraciado*, and then they throw us in jail. We have no choice in the matter. There is absolutely nothing going on now. There is no bombing, there is no fighting in the customs line, there is no tax, there is no terrorism, there is *nothing*."

I supposed that what Agustin Tamargo meant by "no tax" was that there was no community effort, as there had been on occasion in the past, to finance actions against Cuba by collecting from each exile a part of his or her earnings. I did not know what he meant by "no fighting in the customs line," nor, because he seemed at that moment almost mute with disgust, did I ask.

"Nothing," Agustin Tamargo had repeated finally. "Under Reagan."

That there was in Miami under the Reagan administration "nothing" going on was something said to me by many exiles, virtually all of whom spoke as if this "nothing," by which they seemed to mean the absence of more or less daily threats of domestic terror, might be only a temporary suspension, an intermission of uncertain duration in an otherwise familiar production. There was in Miami a general sense that the Reagan administration, largely by the way in which it had managed to convince some exiles that its commitment to "freedom fighters" extended to them, had to some extent co-opted exile action. There was also in Miami a general sense that this was on the Reagan administration's part just another trick of another mirror, another camp in Homestead, say, another interim occupation for Luis Posada Carriles or his manifold doubles, and as such could end predictably. Some exiles spoke with considerable foreboding about what they saw as the community's misplaced wish to believe in the historically doubtful notion that its interests would in the long run coincide with those of Washington. Some exiles suggested that this wish to believe, or rather this willing suspension of disbelief, had not in the past been and was by no means now an open ticket, that there would once again come a point when exile and Washington interests would be seen to diverge, and diverge dramatically.

These exiles saw, when and if this happened, a rekindling of certain familiar frustrations, the unloosing of furies still only provisionally contained; saw, in other words, built into the mirror trick, yet another narrative on which to hang the betrayal, the utilization, the manipulation of *el exilio* by the government of the United States. "I wouldn't be surprised to see some Cubans attempting to re-create political violence in the United States," Daniel Morcate had said the evening we met in Agustin Tamargo's office at WOCN-Union Radio. He had been talking about what he saw as the Reagan administration's reluctance to directly confront Fidel Castro. "There is a very clear danger here that nobody is pointing out. I wouldn't be surprised if other Omega *Siete* groups were emerging."

I had asked Raul Masvidal, the day I saw him in the cool office with the poster that read YOU HAVE NOT CONVERTED A MAN BECAUSE YOU HAVE SILENCED HIM, if he believed that a perceived divergence of exile and Washington interests, a perception in Miami that promises were once again being broken, could bring about a resurgence of the kind of action which had characterized the exile until recently. Raul Masvidal had looked at me, and shrugged. "That kind of action is here today," he had said. I had asked the same question of Luis Lauredo, who was then the president of Raul Masvidal's Miami Savings Bank and was, as the president of Cuban-American Democrats, perhaps the most visible and active member of that 35 percent of the Dade County Cuban electorate who were registered Democrats.

Luis Lauredo had nodded, and then shook his head,

as if the question did not bear contemplation. "I was talking about this last night," he said finally. "With some of the Republicans." We had been sitting across from each other at lunch that day, and I had watched Luis Lauredo fillet a fish before he continued. "We had a kind of gathering," he said then. "And I said to them, 'listen, when it happens, I'll cover your backs.' Because they are going to lose all credibility. It's like a Greek tragedy. That's the way it's going to be. When it happens."

"Those radio guys who attacked me are just looking for ratings," Carlos Luis said one day when I had met him at the Museo Cubano and we had gone around to get something to eat and a coffee, just out of the rain, in the courtyard of the Malaga restaurant on Eighth Street. "Which is why I never answered them. I did a program with Agustin Tamargo, which was good, but I never answered the attacks."

The rain that day had been blowing the bits of colored glass and mirror strung from the tree in the Malaga courtyard and splashing from the eaves overhanging our table and we had been talking in a general way about action of the Left and action of the Right and Carlos Luis had said that he had come to wonder if silence was not the only moral political response. He had a few weeks before, on the twenty-fifth anniversary of the death of Albert Camus, published in *El Herald* a reflection on Camus which had this as its subtext, and it was to this subtext that the "radio guys" had been responding, there apparently being in Miami no subject so remote or abstruse as to rule out its becoming the focus for several hours of invective on AM radio.

"In any event that's the way things are here," Carlos Luis said. "It's very confusing. The guy who attacked me to begin with was totally incapable of discussing Camus's position. Which was a very tragic one. Because the choices Camus had in front of him were not choices at all. Making a choice between terrorism of the Right and terrorism of the Left was incomprehensible to him. Maybe he was right. As time goes by I think that men who were unable to make choices were more right than those who made them. Because there are no clean choices."

Carlos Luis drummed his fingers absently on the wet metal table. It was possible to walk from the Malaga to the bungalow on Seventh Street where Eduardo Arocena had been arrested with the Beretta and the Browning and the AR-15 and the UZI and the target list. It was also possible to walk from the Malaga to the parking lot where Emilio Milian had lost his legs for suggesting on WQBA-*La Cubanísima* that exiles might be working against their own interests by continuing to bomb and assassinate one another on the streets of Miami. On my way to the Museo Cubano de Arte y Cultura that morning I had noticed in a storefront window this poster: ¡NICARAGUA HOY, CUBA MAÑANA! SUPPORT THE FREEDOM FIGHTERS FUND. COMANDO SATURNINO BELTRAN. FREEDOM FIGHTERS FUND,

P.O. BOX 661571, MIAMI SPRINGS FL 33266. JEFATURA MILITAR BRIGADA 2506, P.O. BOX 4086, HIALEAH FL 33014.

This was a year and a half before the Southern Air Transport C-123K carrying Eugene Hasenfus crashed inside Nicaragua. There was between the day of Ronald Reagan's first inauguration and the day the C-123K crashed inside Nicaragua "nothing" going on, but of course there was also "something" going on, something peculiar to the early 1980s in Miami but suggestive of the early 1960s in Miami, something in which certain familiar words and phrases once again figured. It was again possible to hear in Miami about "training," and about air charters and altered manifests and pilots hired for onetime flights from Miami to "somewhere" in Central America. It was again possible to hear in Washington about two-track strategies, about back channels and alternative avenues, about what Robert C. McFarlane, at that time the Reagan administration's National Security Affairs adviser, described variously in the *Washington Post* in 1985 as "a continuity of policy," "a national interest in keeping in touch with what was going on"; a matter of "not breaking faith with the freedom fighters," which in turn came down to "making it clear that the United States believes in what they are doing."

What exactly was involved in making it clear that the United States believed in what the freedom fighters were doing was still, at that time in Miami, the spring of 1985, hard to know in detail, but it was already clear that some of the details were known to some Cubans. There were Cubans around Miami who would later say, about how they happened to end up fighting with the Nicaraguan contras, that they had been during the spring of 1985 "trained" at a camp in the Everglades operated by the Jefatura Militar Brigada 2506. There were Cubans around Miami who would later say, about how they happened to join the Nicaraguan contras, that they had been during the spring of 1985 "recruited" at the little park on Eighth Street a few blocks west of the Malaga. Nothing was happening but certain familiar expectations were being raised, and to speak of choices between terrorism of the Left and terrorism of the Right did not seem, in the courtyard of the Malaga on Eighth Street in Miami during the spring of 1985, an entirely speculative exercise. "There are no choices at all," Carlos Luis said then.

14

WHEN I think now about mirror tricks and what might or might not be built into them, about the ways in which frustrations can be kindled and furies unloosed, I think of Guillermo Novo, called Bill Novo. Guillermo Novo was known to FBI agents and federal prosecutors and the various personnel who made up "terrorist task forces" on the eastern seaboard of the United States as one of the Novo brothers, Ignacio and Guillermo, two exiles who first came to national attention in 1964, when they fired a dud bazooka shell at the United Nations during a speech by Che Guevara. There were certain farcical elements here (the embattled brothers bobbing in a small boat, the shell plopping harmlessly into the East River), and, in a period when Hispanics were seen by many Americans as intrinsically funny, an accent joke, this incident was generally treated tolerantly, a comic footnote to the news. As time went by, however, the names of the Novo brothers began turning up in less comic footnotes, for example this one, on page 93 of volume X of the report made by the House Select Committee on Assassinations on its 1978 investigation of the assassination of John F. Kennedy:

(67) Immunized executive session testimony of Marita Lorenz, May 31, 1978. Hearings before the House Select Committee on Assassinations. Lorenz, who had publicly claimed she was once Castro's mistress (*Miami News*, June 15, 1976), told the committee she was present at a September 1963 meeting in Orlando Bosch's Miami home during which Lee Harvey Oswald, Frank Sturgis, Pedro Diaz Lanz, and Bosch made plans to go to Dallas. . . . She further testified that around November 15, 1963, she, Jerry Patrick Hemming, the Novo brothers, Pedro Diaz Lanz, Sturgis, Bosch, and Oswald traveled in a two-car caravan to Dallas and stayed in a motel where they were contacted by Jack Ruby. There were several rifles and scopes in the motel room . . . Lorenz said she returned to Miami around November 19 or 20. . . . The committee found no evidence to support Lorenz's allegation.

Guillermo Novo himself was among those convicted, in a 1979 trial which rested on the demonstration of connections between the Cuban defendants and DINA, the Chilean secret police, of the assassination in Washington of the former Chilean diplomat Orlando Letelier and of the Institute for Policy Studies researcher who happened to be with him when his car blew up, Ronni Moffitt. This conviction was overturned on appeal (the appellate court ruled that the testimony of two jailhouse informants had been improperly admitted), and in a 1981 retrial, after the federal prosecutors turned down a deal in which the defense offered a plea of guilty on the lesser charge of conspiracy, plus what Guillermo Novo's attorney called "a sweetener," a "guarantee" by Guillermo Novo "to stop all violence by Cuban exiles in the United States," Guillermo Novo was acquitted.

I happened to meet Guillermo Novo in 1985, one Monday morning when I was waiting for someone in the reception room at WRHC-Cadena Azul, Miami, a station the call letters of which stood for Radio Havana Cuba. There was about this meeting nothing of either moment or consequence. A man who introduced himself as "Bill Novo" just appeared beside me, and we exchanged minor biography for a few minutes. He said that he had noticed me reading a letter framed on the wall of the reception room. He said that he was the sales manager for WRHC, and had lived in Miami only three years. He said that he had however lived in the United States since 1954, mostly in New York and New Jersey. He was a small sharp-featured man in a white tropical suit, who in fact spoke English with an accent which suggested New Jersey, and he had a way of materializing and dematerializing sideways, of appearing from and then sidling back into an inner office, which was where he retreated after he gave me his business card, the exchange of cards remaining a more or less fixed ritual in Cuban Miami. GUILLERMO NOVO SAMPOL, the card read. *Gerente de Ventas, WRHC-Cadena Azul.*

That it was possible on a Monday morning in Miami to have so desultory an encounter with one of the

Novo brothers seemed to me, perhaps because I was not yet accustomed to a rhythm in which dealings with DINA and unsupported allegations about Dallas motel rooms could be incorporated into the American business day, remarkable, and later that week I asked an exile acquaintance who was familiar with WRHC if the Guillermo Novo who was the sales manager there was in fact the Guillermo Novo who had been tried in the Letelier assassination. There had been, my acquaintance demurred, "a final acquittal on the Letelier count." But it was, I persisted, the same man. My acquaintance had shrugged impatiently, not as if he thought it best not mentioned, but as if he did not quite see the interest. "Bill Novo has been a man of action," he said. "Yes. Of course."

To be a man of action in Miami was to receive encouragement from many quarters. On the wall of the reception room at WRHC-Cadena Azul, Miami, where the sales manager was Guillermo Novo and an occasional commentator was Fidel and Raúl Castro's estranged sister Juanita and the host of the most popular talk show was Felipe Rivero, whose family had from 1832 until 1960 published the powerful *Diario de la Marina* in Havana and who would in 1986, after a controversy fueled by his insistence that the Holocaust had not occurred but had been fabricated "to defame and divide the German people," move from WRHC to WOCN, there hung in 1985 a framed letter, the letter Guillermo Novo had mentioned when he first materialized that Monday morning. This letter, which was dated October 1983 and signed by the President of the United States, read:

> I learned from Becky Dunlop [presumably Becky Norton Dunlop, a White House aide who later followed Edwin Meese to the Justice Department] about the outstanding work being done at WRHC. Many of your listeners have also been in touch, praising your news coverage and your editorials. Your talented staff deserves special commendation for keeping your listeners well-informed.

> I've been particularly pleased, of course, that you have been translating and airing a Spanish version of my weekly talks. This is important because your signal reaches the people of Cuba, whose rigidly controlled government media suppress any news Castro and his communist henchmen do not want them to know. WRHC is performing a great service for all its listeners. Keep up the good work, and God bless you.

> [signed] RONALD REAGAN

At the time I first noticed it on the WRHC wall, and attracted Guillermo Novo's attention by reading it, this letter interested me because I had the week before been looking back through the administration's arguments for Radio Martí, none of which, built as they were on the figure of beaming light into utter darkness, had alluded to these weekly talks which the people of Cuba appeared to be getting on WRHC-Cadena Azul, Miami. Later the letter interested me because I had begun reading back through the weekly radio talks themselves, and had come across one from 1978 in which Ronald Reagan, not yet president, had expressed his doubt that either the Pinochet government or the indicted "Cuban anti-Castro exiles," one of whom had been Guillermo Novo, had anything to do with the Letelier assassination.

Ronald Reagan had wondered instead ("I don't know the answer, but it is a question worth asking . . .") if Orlando Letelier's "connections with Marxists and far-left causes" might not have set him up for assassination, caused him to be, as the script for this talk put it, "murdered by his own masters." Here was the scenario: "Alive," Ronald Reagan had reasoned in 1978, Orlando Letelier "could be compromised; dead he could become a martyr. And the left didn't lose a minute in making him one." Actually this version of the Letelier assassination had first been advanced by Senator Jesse Helms (R-N.C.), who had advised his colleagues on the Senate floor that it was not "plausible" to suspect the Pinochet government in the Letelier case, because terrorism was "most often an organized tool of the left," but the Reagan reworking was interesting on its own, a way of speaking, later to become familiar, in which events could be revised as they happened into illustrations of ideology.

"There was no blacklist of Hollywood," Ronald Reagan told Robert Scheer of the *Los Angeles Times* during the 1980 campaign. "The blacklist in Hollywood, if there was one, was provided by the communists." "I'm going to voice a suspicion now that I've never said aloud before," Ronald Reagan told thirty-six high-school students in Washington in 1983 about death squads in El Salvador. "I wonder if all of this is right wing, or if those guerrilla forces have not realized that by infiltrating into the city of San Salvador and places like that, they can get away with these violent acts, helping to try and bring down the government, and the right wing will be blamed for it." "New intelligence shows," Ronald Reagan told his Saturday radio listeners in March of 1986, by way of explaining why he was asking Congress to provide "the Nicaraguan freedom fighters" with what he called "the means to fight back," that "Tomás Borge, the communist interior minister, is engaging in a brutal campaign to bring the freedom fighters into discredit. You see, Borge's communist operatives dress in freedom fighter uniforms, go into the countryside and murder and mutilate ordinary Nicaraguans."

Such stories were what David Gergen, when he was the White House communications director, had once called "a folk art," the President's way of "trying to tell us how society works." Other members of the White House staff had characterized these stories as the President's "notions," casting them in the genial framework of random avuncular musings, but they were something more than that. In the first place they were never random, but systematic, and rather energetically so. The stories were told to a single point. The language in which the stories were told was not that of political argument but of advertising ("New intelligence shows . . ." and "Now it has been learned . . ." and, a construction that got my attention in a 1984 address to the National Religious Broadcasters, "Medical science doctors confirm . . ."), of the sales pitch.

This was not just a vulgarity of diction. When someone speaks of Orlando Letelier as "murdered by his own masters," or of the WRHC signal reaching a people denied information by "Castro and his communist henchmen," or of the "freedom fighter uniforms" in which the "communist operatives" of the "communist interior minister" disguise themselves, that person is not arguing a case, but counting instead on the willingness of the listener to enter what Hannah Arendt called, in a discussion of propaganda, "the gruesome quiet of an entirely imaginary world." On the morning I met Guillermo Novo in the reception room at WRHC-Cadena Azul I copied the framed commendation from the White House into my notebook, and later typed it out and pinned it to my own office wall, an aide-mémoire to the distance between what is said in the high ether of Washington, which is about the making of those gestures and the sending of those messages and the drafting of those positions which will serve to maintain that imaginary world, about two-track strategies and alternative avenues and Special Groups (Augmented), about "not breaking faith" and "making it clear," and what is heard on the ground in Miami, which is about consequences.

•

In many ways Miami remains our most graphic lesson in consequences. "I can assure you that this flag will be returned to this brigade in a free Havana," John F. Kennedy said at the Orange Bowl in 1962 (the "supposed promise," the promise "not in the script," the promise "made in the emotion of the day"), meaning it as an abstraction, the rhetorical expression of a collective wish; a kind of poetry, which of course makes nothing happen. "We will not permit the Soviets and their henchmen in Havana to deprive others of their freedom," Ronald Reagan said at the Dade County Auditorium in 1983 (2,500 people inside, 60,000 outside, 12 standing ovations and a *pollo asado* lunch at La Esquina de Tejas with Jorge Mas Canosa and 203 other provisional loyalists), and then Ronald Reagan, the first American president since John F. Kennedy to visit Miami in search of Cuban support, added this: "Someday, Cuba itself will be free."

This was of course just more poetry, another rhetorical expression of the same collective wish, but Ronald Reagan, like John F. Kennedy before him, was speaking here to people whose historical experience has not been that poetry makes nothing happen. On one of the first evenings I spent in Miami I sat at midnight over *carne con papas* in an art-filled condominium in one of the Arquitectonica buildings on Brickell Avenue and listened to several exiles talk about the relationship of what was said in Washington to what was done in Miami. These exiles were all well-educated. They were well-read, well-traveled, comfortable citizens of a larger world than that of either Miami or Washington, with well-cut blazers and French dresses and interests in New York and Madrid and Mexico. Yet what was said that evening in the expensive condominium overlooking Biscayne Bay proceeded from an almost primitive helplessness, a regressive fury at having been, as these exiles saw it, repeatedly used and repeatedly betrayed by the government of the United States. "Let me tell you something," one of them said. "They talk about 'Cuban terrorists.' The guys they call 'Cuban terrorists' are the guys they trained."

This was not, then, the general exile complaint about a government which might have taken up their struggle but had not. This was something more specific, a complaint that the government in question had in fact taken up *la lucha*, but for its own purposes, and, in what these exiles saw as a pattern of deceit stretching back through six administrations, to its own ends. The pattern, as they saw it, was one in which the government of the United States had repeatedly encouraged or supported exile action and then, when policy shifted and such action became an embarrassment, a discordant note in whatever message Washington was sending that month or that year, had discarded the exiles involved, had sometimes not only discarded them but, since the nature of *la lucha* was essentially illegal, turned them in, set them up for prosecution; positioned them, as it were, for the fall.

They mentioned, as many exiles did, the Omega 7 prosecutions. They mentioned, as many exiles did, the Cuban burglars at the Watergate, who were told, because so many exiles had come by that time to distrust the CIA, that the assignment at hand was not just CIA, but straight from the White House. They mentioned the case of Jose Elias de la Torriente, a respected exile leader who had been, in the late 1960s, recruited by the CIA to lend his name and his prestige to what was set forth as a new plan to overthrow Fidel Castro, the "Work Plan for Liberation," or the Torriente Plan.

Money had once again been raised, and expectations. The entire attention of *el exilio* had for a time been focused on the Torriente Plan, a diversion of energy which, as years passed and nothing happened, suggested to many that what the plan may have been from its inception was just another ad hoc solution to the disposal problem, another mirror trick. Jose Elias de la Torriente had been called, by a frustrated community once again left with nowhere to go, a traitor. Jose Elias de la Torriente had been called a CIA stooge. Jose Elias de la Torriente had finally been, at age seventy, as he sat in his house in Coral Gables watching *The Robe* on television about nine o'clock on the evening of Good Friday, 1974, assassinated, shot through the venetian blind on a window by someone, presumably an exile, who claimed the kill in the name "Zero."

This had, in the telling at the dinner table, the sense of a situation played out to its Aristotelian end, of that inexorable Caribbean progress from cause to effect which I later came to see as central to the way Miami thought about itself. Miami stories tended to have endings. The cannon onstage tended to be fired. One of those who spoke most ardently that evening was a quite beautiful young woman in a white jersey dress, a lawyer, active in Democratic politics in Miami. This dinner in the condominium overlooking Biscayne Bay took place in March of 1985, and the woman in the white jersey dress was María Elena Prío Durán, the child who flew into exile in March of 1952 with her father's foreign minister, her father's minister of the interior, her father, her sister, and her mother, the equally beautiful woman in the hat with the fishnet veiling.

I recall watching María Elena Prío Durán that night as she pushed back her hair and reached across the table for a cigarette. This, like the lunch in the Malaga courtyard when Carlos Luis had talked about Albert Camus and the choice between terror of the Right and terror of the Left, was a long time before the C-123K carrying Eugene Hasenfus fell from the sky inside Nicaragua. This was a long time before Eugene Hasenfus mentioned the names of the 2506 members already in place at Ilopango. NICARAGUA HOY, CUBA MAÑANA. Let me tell you about Cuban terrorists, another of the exiles at dinner that night, a prominent Miami architect named Raúl Rodríguez, was saying at the end of the table. Cuba never grew plastique. Cuba grew tobacco. Cuba grew sugarcane. Cuba never grew C-4. María Elena Prío Durán lit the cigarette and immediately crushed it out. C-4, Raúl Rodríguez said, and he slammed his palm down on the white tablecloth as he said it, grew here.

FOUR

15

EARLY on the morning of April 19, 1961, when it was clear in Washington that the invasion then underway at Playa Girón had failed, President John F. Kennedy dispatched Adolf A. Berle of the State Department and Arthur M. Schlesinger, Jr., of the White House staff to Miami, to meet with what had been until a few hours before the projected provisional government for a post-Castro Cuba, the Cuban Revolutionary Council, the members of which were being kept temporarily incommunicado in a CIA barracks at the Opa-Locka Airport. "A couple of hours into our meeting with the Kennedy people, I got the feeling that we were being taken for a ride," one member of the council later told the exile sociologist José Llanes, who quoted but did not name him in *Cuban Americans: Masters of Survival.* "The *comierda* [Llanes translates this as "shit face"] they sent me was only worried about the political popularity of their man." In *A Thousand Days,* Arthur M. Schlesinger, Jr., described his and Adolf Berle's thoughts during the same meeting: "Our hearts sank as we walked out for a moment into the dazzling sun. How could we notify the Cubans that there was no hope, that their

sons were abandoned for captivity or death—and at
the same time dissuade them from public denunciation
of the CIA and the United States government?"

What is interesting here is how closely these two
views of the meeting at the Opa-Locka Airport, the
Miami and the Washington, appear to coincide. The
problem that April morning for Schlesinger and Berle,
Schlesinger seems himself to suggest, was one of presentation, of damage control, which is another way of
saying that they were worried about the political popularity of their man. The solution, as they devised it,
was to take the exiles for a literal ride: to fly them immediately to Washington and give them an afternoon
audience in the Oval Office, a meeting at which the
members of the Cuban Revolutionary Council (several of whom had sons or brothers on the beachhead
that day) would sit by the fireplace and hear the
President speak of the responsibilities of leadership, of
the struggle against communism on its many fronts
and of his own commitment to the "eventual" freedom of Cuba; a meeting which in fact took place, and
at which, according to Schlesinger, the President spoke
"slowly and thoughtfully" ("I had never seen the
President more impressive"), and the members of the
Cuban Revolutionary Council had been, "in spite of
themselves," "deeply moved." Here, the Washington
and the Miami views no longer coincide: the recita-
tive of seduction and betrayal from which Miami took
its particular tone was in a key Washington failed
then to hear, and does still.

•

On April 10, 1984, midway through yet another administration during which it was periodically suggested that the struggle against communism on its many fronts included a commitment to the eventual freedom of Cuba, an unexceptional Tuesday morning during a week in which *The New York Times* reported that the mining of Nicaraguan harbors had "rekindled doubts in Congress and among some officials in the Reagan administration about the extensive use of covert activities to advance United States interests in Central America," Ronald Reagan, the fortieth President of the United States, was presented to be photographed in the following Washington settings: greeting President Salvador Jorge Blanco of the Dominican Republic on the South Grounds of the White House (10:00 A.M.), conferring with President Salvador Jorge Blanco of the Dominican Republic in the Oval Office of the White House (10:30 A.M.), and placing a telephone call from the Oval Office to the *Challenger* space shuttle, an event covered only by a pool camera crew but piped live into the press briefing room in the West Wing of the White House:

THE PRESIDENT: Hello, Bob—these calls—
ASTRONAUT CRIPPEN: Good afternoon, Mr. President. Thank you very much for speaking with us.
THE PRESIDENT: Well, these calls between the two of us are becoming a habit. I promise you, though, I won't reverse the charges. Over.
ASTRONAUT CRIPPEN: I don't think I can afford them, Mr. President. (*Laughter.*)

THE PRESIDENT: Well, once again, I'm calling to congratulate you and the rest of the crew aboard the *Challenger* there on an historic mission. The retrieval of the Solar Max satellite this morning was just great. And you and the crew demonstrated once again just how versatile the space shuttle is and what we can accomplish by having a team in space and on the ground. I know you'll agree that those folks at the Goddard Space Flight Center did a fantastic job maneuvering the satellite for you. And, Terry, I guess you made one long reach for man this morning when you snapped that satellite with the fifty-foot robot arms. And George and Jim, you've done fine work as well. The pictures sent back of you working in space are spectacular. They're also a little scary for those of us who are sitting comfortably anchored to the earth. But, Bob, I understand that satellite you have on board would cost us about two hundred million dollars to build at today's prices, so if you can't fix it up there, would you mind bringing it back? Over.

ASTRONAUT CRIPPEN: Well, we—we're going to do our best to repair it tomorrow, sir, and if, for some reason, that is unsuccessful, which we don't think it will be, we will be able to return it. We certainly concur with all of your remarks. The *Challenger* and its sister ships are magnificent flying machines and I think that they can make a significant road into space in regard to repair and servicing of satellites. And we believe this is the initial step. I would also like to concur with your remarks regarding the people up at Goddard who managed to put this satellite back in a configuration that we could retrieve it after the little problem we ran into the other day. Those people and the people in Houston and everybody that worked on it truly made this recovery possible. It is a team effort all the way. It so happens we get to do the fun part.

THE PRESIDENT: Well, let me tell you, you're all a team that has made all Americans very proud of what you're doing up there, and what the future bodes for all of us with regard to this opening up of that great frontier of space. And, seriously, I just want to again say how proud we all are of all of you, and congratulations to you all. Have a safe mission, a safe trip home, and God bless all of you. I'll sign out and let you get on with your chores.

There was at first a silence in the West Wing briefing room. "Sign off," someone said then. "Not 'sign out,' 'sign *off*.' "

" 'And, seriously'?" someone else said. "What does that mean, 'And, seriously'?"

This telephone call between the Oval Office and space lasted four minutes, between 12:01 P.M. and 12:05 P.M., and was followed immediately in the briefing room by a report on the meeting between President Reagan and President Salvador Jorge Blanco of the Dominican Republic, or rather on that part of the meeting which had taken place after the pool camera crew left the Oval Office. This report was delivered by Assistant Secretary of State for Inter-American Affairs Langhorne Motley ("This briefing is on background and is attributable to 'a senior Administration official,' " a voice on the loudspeaker had advised before Langhorne Motley appeared), who said that the meeting between the two presidents, dealing with how best to oppose those who were "destabilizing" and "working against the forces of democracy" in Central America, had in fact ended when the pool camera crew was escorted back into the Oval Office to light the phone call to the astronauts.

On this unexceptional Tuesday midway through his administration the President of the United States was lit and photographed as well in the Old Executive Office Building at a ceremony marking Fair Housing Month (1:30 P.M.); in the Rose Garden signing H.R. 4072, the Agricultural Programs Adjustments Act of 1984 (3:45 P.M.); in the Oval Office signing H.R. 4206, an amendment to the Internal Revenue Code (4:30 P.M.); in the Oval Office greeting the board of directors of the Electronics Industries Association (4:45 P.M.), and, later, in three State Dinner situations: descending the Grand Staircase at 7:45 P.M., toasting President Jorge Blanco in the State Dining Room at 9:15 P.M., and, at 10:35 P.M., addressing his guests, including Wayne Newton and his date, Brooke Shields and her mother, Oscar de la Renta, Pilar Crespi and Tommy Lasorda, in the East Room. Of the day's events, some had been open to

the White House press corps at large; others limited
to the camera crews and a few pool print reporters,
who duly submitted their reports for distribution by
the White House press office:

POOL REPORT, Reagan and Fair Housing:
The ceremony was attended by representatives
of civil rights and fair housing groups, builders
and realtors who cooperated with HUD to make
sure fair housing law works. The room was half
full. Secretary Pierce presented several awards.
One celebrity present, Phyllis Hyman, Celebri-
ties for Fair Housing. She is a Broadway musical
star. The President stood under a sign:

> Fair Housing
> I support it
> President Reagan supports it
> All America Needs It.

He spoke for about five minutes.

—*Vic Ostrowidzki*
Hearst Newspapers.

POOL REPORT, Meeting with President Jorge
Blanco in the Oval Office: The two presidents sat
side by side, exchanging pleasantries. When we
were brought in, President Jorge Blanco was in
the process of telling President Reagan about his
prior visit to the U.S. and that this trip was "an
extension of that visit." At one point, President
Reagan said "when you were speaking this morn-

ing the planes were coming over. They are a big problem at the time they take off. They come every three minutes apart. There is a great deal of public sentiment about that." We never found out what that "sentiment" is because the President suddenly looked up, saw us staring at him expectantly and stopped in mid-sentence. To a question "Are you going to discuss the mining of ports?" Reagan responded "no questions at photo opportunity" and L. Speakes shouted, "lights out."

　　—*Vic Ostrowidzki*
　　Hearst Newspapers.

"Almost everything we do is determined by whether we think it will get on the network news shows in the evening," Larry Speakes, at that time the chief White House spokesman, was quoted as saying in an Associated Press story later that week. "We obviously would like to highlight the positive story of the day for the President," Michael Deaver, then White House deputy chief of staff, said in the same story, which was about his efforts to get the President photographed in more "spontaneous" settings, for example making a surprise visit to Monticello and eating a hot dog in the Baltimore Orioles' dugout. "I think you have to give credit to Mike Deaver and to Bill Henkel, our chief advance man, for setting the scene at the demilitarized zone in South Korea last December," David Gergen had said not long before, to *The New York Times*, when asked for highlights of his three-year tenure as White House director of communications.

"The pictures said as much as anything the President could say." He was talking about those still photographs and pieces of film which had shown the President, in the course of a visit to South Korea, at the 38th parallel, with field glasses and battle helmet. "Audiences," David Gergen had added, "will listen to you more if they see the President in an interesting setting. Their memory of the event will be more vivid. We spend a fair amount of time thinking about that."

In Washington, then, midway through the Reagan administration, it was taken for granted that the White House schedule should be keyed to the daily network feeds. It was taken for granted that the efforts of the White House staff should be directed toward the setting of interesting scenes. It was taken for granted that the overriding preoccupation of the White House staff (the subject of a senior staff meeting every morning, an additional meeting every Wednesday, a meeting on foreign coverage every Thursday, and a "brainstorming" lunch at Blair House every Friday) should be the invention of what had come to be called "talking points," the production of "guidance"; the creation and strategic management of what David Gergen had characterized as "the story line we are trying to develop that week or that month."

The story's protagonist, the President himself, was said, even then, to be "detached," or "disengaged from the decision-making process," a condition presented, in the accepted cipher, as an asset in itself: here was a protagonist who "delegated authority," who "refused to get mired in details," attractive managerial skills that suggested a superior purchase on the larger picture. Patrick Buchanan reported that the President had "mastered the art of compartmentalization." Morton Kondracke wondered when "Mr. Reagan's opponents would stop underestimating him and would begin to realize that he has to be pretty smart—even if his intellect does not work like an academic's—and that he has to have a grasp of the large issues confronting the country, even if he has a disconcerting way of not bothering with the details."

"You don't need to know who's playing on the White House tennis court to be a good president," James Baker had liked to say when he was chief of staff. "A president has many roles," White House aides frequently advised reporters, a construct sufficiently supple, even silky, to cover any missed cue, dropped stitch, irreconcilable contradiction or frank looniness that came to light. "I don't have any problem with a reporter or a news person who says the President is uninformed on this issue or that issue," David Gergen had said in the course of a 1984 discussion sponsored by the American Enterprise Institute. "I don't think any of us would challenge that. I do have a problem with the singular focus on this, as if that's the only standard by which we ought to judge a president. What we learned in the last administration was how little having an encyclopedic grasp of all the facts has to do with governing."

Such professed faith in the mystery of "governing," in the ineffable contract that was said to exist between the President and the people (often so called), was only part of what was taken for granted, midway through the Reagan administration. It was also taken for granted that the presidency had been redefined as an essentially passive role, that of "communicator," or "leader," which had been redefined in turn to mean that person whose simple presence before a camera was believed to command support for the policy proposed. It was taken for granted that the key to understanding the policy could be found in the shifts of position and ambition among the President's men. It was taken for granted that the President himself was, if not exactly absent when Larry Speakes ordered lights out, something less than entirely present, the condition expressed even then by the code word "incurious." It was taken for granted, above all, that the reporters and camera operators and still photographers and sound technicians and lighting technicians and producers and electricians and on-camera correspondents showed up at the White House because the President did, and it was also taken for granted, the more innovative construction, that the President showed up at the White House because the reporters and camera operators and still photographers and sound technicians and lighting technicians and producers and electricians and on-camera correspondents did.

In Washington midway through the Reagan administration many things were taken for granted, I learned during time spent there during two consecutive springs, that were not necessarily taken for granted in less abstract venues. I recall talking about

the adminstration's Central American policy, one afternoon in 1984, to David Gergen, and being struck
not exactly by what he said but by the way in which
he said it, by the terms in which he described what
he called the "several stages" of "the same basic policy." The terms David Gergen used that afternoon
were exclusively those of presentation. He spoke first
of "the very hard line taken in the spring of 1981,"
a time for "a lot of focus, a lot of attention." He
spoke of a period, later the same spring, when "it
wasn't looking good, so we kind of moved it back."
He spoke of a later period, in 1982, "when some people in the administration thought it could become
serious," a time when "we thought we should start
laying the groundwork, building some public support
for what we might have to do"; a time, then, for
moving it not "back" but forward. "I would say this
continued to the end of 1983," David Gergen had
said finally that afternoon in 1984, his voice trailing
off and perhaps his attention: this was to him a familiar chronology, and like many people whose business was the art of the possible he appeared to have
only a limited interest in even the most recent past.
"Then some people began to see it as a negative issue,
and to ask why do we want to make Central America
front and center again, so there was an effort to pull
it back."

David Gergen had worked in the White House
during three administrations, and acquired during the
course of them an entire vocabulary of unattributable
nods and acquiescent silences, a diction that tended

to evaporate like smoke, but the subtext of what he was saying on this spring afternoon in 1984 seemed clear, and to suggest a view of the government of the United States, from someone who had labored at its exact heart for nine of the preceding thirteen years, not substantively different from the view of the government of the United States held by those Cubans to whom I later talked in Miami: the government of the United States was in this view one for which other parts of the world, in this instance Central America, existed only as "issues." In some seasons, during some administrations and in the course of some campaigns, Central America had seemed a useful issue, one to which "focus" and "attention" could profitably be drawn. In other seasons it had seemed a "negative" issue, one which failed to meet, for whatever reason, the test of "looking good."

In all seasons, however, it remained a potentially valuable asset in this business of the art of the possible, and not just an ordinary special-interest, domestic asset, but a national security card, a jeopardy chip, a marker that carried with it the glamour of possible military action, the ultimate interesting setting. As such, it would ideally remain on the board, sometimes available to be moved "back," sometimes available to be moved (whenever the moment seemed to call for a show of determination and resolution, a demonstration, say, of standing tall) "front and center." That each move left a certain residue on the board was what some people in Washington had called their disposal problem, and some people in Miami their betrayal.

16

THERE were in Washington during the Reagan administration a small but significant number of people for whom the commitment to American involvement in Central America did not exist exclusively as an issue, a marker to be moved sometimes front, sometimes back. These were people for whom the commitment to American involvement in Central America was always front, in fact "the" front, the battleground on which, as Ronald Reagan had put it in his second inaugural address and on many occasions before and after, "human freedom" was "on the march." These were people who had believed early on and even formulated what was eventually known as the Reagan Doctrine, people committed to the idea that "rollback," or the reversal of Soviet power which had been part of the rhetoric of the American Right since at least the Eisenhower administration, could now be achieved by supporting guerrilla resistance movements around the world; people who believed that, in the words of *A New Inter-American Policy for the Eighties*, a fifty-three-page policy proposal issued in the summer of 1980 by the Council for Inter-American Security, "containment of the Soviet Union is not enough. Detente is dead.

Survival demands a new U.S. foreign policy. America must seize the initiative or perish. For World War III is almost over."

A New Inter-American Policy for the Eighties, usually referred to, because the discussions from which it derived took place in New Mexico, as the Santa Fe statement or the Santa Fe document, was a curious piece of work, less often talked about in this country than in Managua and Havana, where it was generally regarded, according to Edward Cody in the *Washington Post* and Christopher Dickey in *With the Contras*, as a blueprint to Reagan administration intentions in the hemisphere. In fact what seemed most striking about the Santa Fe document was not that it was read in, but that it might have been written in, Managua or Havana. As a document prepared by Americans it seemed not quite authentic, perhaps a piece of "black propaganda," something put forth clandestinely by a foreign government but purporting to be, in the interests of encouraging anti-American sentiment, American. The grasp on the language was not exactly that of native English speakers. The tone of the preoccupations was not exactly that of the American foreign policy establishment:

> During the last several years, United States policy toward the other nations within the Western Hemisphere has been one of hoping for the best. Too often it has been a policy described by The Committee of Santa Fe as "anxious accommodation," as if we would prevent the political colora-

tion of Latin America to red crimson by an American-prescribed tint of pale pink. Whatever the pedigree of American policy toward our immediate neighbors, it is not working. . . .

The policies of the past decade regarding arms sales and security assistance are totally bankrupt and discredited at home and abroad. . . . Combining our arsenal of weaponry with the manpower of the Americas, we can create a free hemisphere of the Americas, that can withstand Soviet-Cuban aggression. . . .

U.S. policy formation must insulate itself from propaganda appearing in the general and specialized media which is inspired by forces specifically hostile to the United States. . . .

U.S. foreign policy must begin to counter (not react against) liberation theology as it is utilized in Latin America by the "liberation theology" clergy. . . .

A campaign to capture the Ibero-American intellectual elite through the media of radio, television, books, articles and pamphlets, plus grants, fellowships and prizes must be initiated. For consideration and recognition are what most intellectuals crave, and such a program would attract them. The U.S. effort must reflect the true sentiments of the American people, not the narrow spectrum of New York and Hollywood. . . .

Human rights, which is a culturally and politically relative concept . . . must be abandoned and replaced by a non-interventionist policy of political and ethical realism. The culturally and ethically relative nature of notions of human rights is clear from the fact that Argentines, Brazilians and Chileans find it repugnant that the United States, which legally sanctions the liquidation of more than 1,000,000 unborn children each year, exhibits moral outrage at the killing of a terrorist who bombs and machine-guns innocent citizens. What, they ask, about the human rights of the victims of left-wing terrorism? U.S. policy-makers must discard the illusion that anyone who picks up a Molotov cocktail in the name of human rights is human-righteous. . . .

Havana must be held to account for its policies of aggression against its sister states in the Americas. Among those steps will be the establishment of a Radio Free Cuba, under open U.S. government sponsorship, which will beam objective information to the Cuban people that, among other things, details the costs of Havana's unholy alliance with Moscow. If propaganda fails, a war of national liberation against Castro must be launched.

The five authors of *A New Inter-American Policy for the Eighties*, who called themselves "The Committee of Santa Fe," were all well-known on the Right, regulars on the boards and letterheads of the various conservative lobbies and foundations around Washington. There was Lynn Francis Bouchey of the Council for Inter-American Security. There was David C. Jordan, a professor of government at the University of Virginia and the coauthor of *Nationalism in Contemporary Latin America.* There was Lieutenant General Gordon Sumner, Jr., at one time chairman of the Inter-American Defense Board and later, during the Reagan administration, special adviser to the assistant secretary of state for inter-American affairs. There was Roger Fontaine, formerly the director for Latin America at the Georgetown University Center for Strategic and International Studies and later, during the Reagan administration, a Latin American specialist at the National Security Council. There was, finally, Lewis Tambs, who had worked in Caracas and Maracaibo as a pipeline engineer for Creole Petroleum and was later, during the Reagan administration, appointed as ambassador first to Colombia, then to Costa Rica, where, as he eventually told both the Tower Commission and the select committees investigating arms shipments to the contras, he understood himself to have been charged with the task of opening a southern front for the Nicaraguan resistance.

According to these men and to that small but significant group of people who thought as they did, the people with whom they shared the boards and letterheads of the various conservative lobbies and foundations around Washington, the "crisis" facing the United States in Central America was "metaphysical." The war was "for the minds of mankind." What the Santa Fe document had called "ideo-politics" would "prevail." These were not people, as time passed and men like James Baker and Michael Deaver and David Gergen moved into the White House, men who understood that the distinction between a crisis and no crisis was one of "perception," or "setting the scene," particularly close to the center of power. They were all, in varying degrees, ideologues, people who had seized or been seized by an idea, and, as such, they were to the White House only sometimes useful.

Where they were useful, of course, was in voicing the concerns not only of the American Right but in some inchoate way of the President himself: with the Santa Fe document they had even managed, in the rather astonishing context of a foreign policy proposal, to drill through their own discussion of the Roldós Doctrine and the Rio Treaty and into that molten core where "New York" was the problem, and "Hollywood," and women who liquidated their unborn children, the very magma of resentment on which Ronald Reagan's appeal had seemed always to float. Where these conservative spokesmen were less useful, where they were in fact profoundly not useful, was in recognizing when the moment had come to move the war for the minds of mankind "back," or anywhere but "front"; in accepting a place in the wings when the stage was set for a different scene. They tended to lack an appreciation of the full script. They tended not to wait backstage without constant diversion, and it was precisely the contriving of such diversion which seemed to most fully engage, as time went by, the attention and energy of the Reagan White House.

Sometimes a diversion was referred to as "sending a signal." The White House Outreach Working Group on Central America, or, as it was sometimes called, "Operation Outreach," was a "signal," one of several efforts conceived during 1982 and 1983 when the White House decided that the time was right for, as David Gergen put it, "laying the groundwork," for "building some public support for what we might have to do"; for, in the words of an April 1982 National Security Planning Group document, addressing the "public affairs dimension of the Central American problem" through a "concerted public information effort." There was at first talk about something called "Project Truth." "Project Truth" melted almost immediately into the "Office of Public Diplomacy," which was set up in 1982, put under the direction of a former Miami city official named Otto Juan Reich (who was born in Havana, in 1945, but whose parents had emigrated to Cuba from Austria), and charged with a task which appeared in practice to consist largely of disseminating classified and sometimes "unevaluated" information ("unevaluated" information was that which had not been and in some cases could not be corroborated) tending to support administration contentions about Nicaragua and El Salvador.

The Office of Public Diplomacy, although at the time of its inception controlled by the White House and the National Security Council, was technically under the aegis of the State Department. At the White House itself there was the "Office of Public Liaison" (the word "public," in this administration even more than in others, tended to suggest a sell in progress), and it was out of this "Office of Public Liaison," then under the direction of Faith Ryan Whittlesey, that the White House Outreach Working Group on Central America emerged. The idea was, on its face, straightforward enough: a series of regular briefings, open to the public, at which the administration could "tell its story" about Central America, "make the case" for its interests there. "We hadn't in a systematic way communicated the facts to people who were perfectly willing to do more themselves to support the President but just didn't have access to the information," Faith Ryan Whittlesey told the *Los Angeles Times* not long after the Outreach Working Group began meeting, every Wednesday afternoon at two-thirty, in Room 450 of the Old Executive Office Building. "All the people need is information. They know what to do with it."

The briefings themselves were somewhat less straightforward. For one thing they were not, or the first forty-five of them were not, open to the public

at all: they were not open, most specifically, to reporters, the very people who might have been expected to carry the information to a larger number
of Americans than were apt to arrange their Wednesday afternoons to include a two-hour session in Room
450 of the Old Executive Office Building. Even after
the Outreach briefings had finally been opened to
the press, in April of 1984, the White House Office
of Public Liaison seemed notably uninterested in talking to reporters: I recall one week in Washington
during which, from Monday through Friday, I placed
repeated calls to Faith Ryan Whittlesey's office, each
time giving my affiliation (I had been asked by a
magazine to write a piece about the Reagan administration, and given a kind of introduction to the White
House by the magazine's Washington editor), de-
tailing my interest in discussing the Outreach program, and expressing my hope that either Mrs. Whittlesey or someone else in the White House Office of
Public Liaison could find a moment to return my call.

Neither Mrs. Whittlesey nor anyone else in the
White House Office of Public Liaison did find such
a moment, not any day that week or ever, which did
not at the time unduly surprise me: it had been my
experience that people who worked for the government in Washington were apt to regard anyone who
did not work for the government in Washington as
a supplicant, a citizen to whom the rightful order must
constantly be made clear, and that one of the several
ways of asserting this rightful order was by not returning telephone calls. In other words I thought of

these unreturned calls to Faith Ryan Whittlesey as unspecific, evidence only of an attitude that came with the particular autointoxication of the territory. Not until later, after I had managed to attend a few Outreach meetings, febrile afternoons in 1984 and 1985 during which the United States was seen to be waging the war for the minds of mankind not only against the Sandinistas in Nicaragua and the FMLN in El Salvador and the Castro government in Cuba and the Machel government in Mozambique but also against its own Congress, against its own State Department, against some members (James Baker, Michael Deaver) of its own executive branch, and, most pointedly, against its own press, did it occur to me that this particular series of unreturned telephone calls may well have been specific; that there was in the White House Outreach Working Group on Central America an inherent peculiarity perhaps best left, from the White House point of view, undiscussed.

This peculiarity was at first hard to assimilate. It did not exactly derive from the actual briefings, most of which seemed, however casually inflammatory, however apt to veer vertiginously out of Central America and into Mozambique and Angola and denunciations of Chester Crocker on the African desk at the State Department, standard enough. There was Francis X. Gannon, then adviser to Alejandro Orfila at the Organization of American States, on "Central America: A Democratic Perspective." ("Somebody at OAS said about the Kissinger Commission, 'What should we send them?' And I said, 'Send them a map.' ") There was General Alexander M. Haig, Jr., on "The Imperatives of Central America in Perspective" ("My opinion of what is happening in Central America is this: the jury is still out"), a raconteur's version of American foreign policy during which General Haig referred to one of its principals with doubtful bonhomie ("So Henry had one of those Germanic tantrums of his . . ."), to another by a doubtful diminutive ("I again will not make any apologies for recounting the fact that I was opposed to covert action in 1981, as Jeannie Kirkpatrick will tell you . . ."), and to himself in the third person, as "Al Haig," or just "Haig."

Some briefings got a little closer to the peculiarity. I recall one particularly heady Outreach meeting, in 1985, at which one of the speakers was a fantast named Jack Wheeler, who liked to say that *Izvestia* had described him as an "ideological gangster" ("When the Soviet Union calls me that, it means I'm starting to get under their skin") but was identified on the afternoon's program simply as "Philosopher, Traveler, and Founder of the Freedom Research Foundation." As it happened I had heard Jack Wheeler before, at a Conservative Political Action Conference session on "Rolling Back the Soviet Empire," where he had received a standing ovation after suggesting that copies of the Koran be smuggled into the Soviet Union to "stimulate an Islamic revival" and the subsequent "death of a thousand cuts," and I was already familiar not only with many of his exploits but with his weird and rather punitive enthusiasm.

Jack Wheeler had recently been with the *mujaheddin* in Afghanistan. He had recently been with Jonas Savimbi in Angola. He had recently been with the insurgents in Cambodia, and Mozambique. He knew of a clandestine radio operating in South Yemen. He saw the first stirrings of democratic liberation in Suriname. He had of course recently been with the contras in Nicaragua, and had, that afternoon in Room 450 of the Old Executive Office Building, brought a few slides to share.

"This is Charley." Jack Wheeler had chuckled as the first slide appeared on the screen. "Charley is a contra. He only looks like he's going to kill you. Actually he's a very nice guy. I told him he looked like Chuck Berry." The slide had changed, and there on the screen was Jack Wheeler himself, his arm around Enrique Bermúdez, the FDN comandante who had been until 1979 a colonel in the Somoza National Guard: "Enrique Bermúdez is convinced—he told me—that only the physical defeat of the Sandinistas will remove the cancer of Soviet-Cuban imperialism and Marxism from Central America." Another slide, this one of a full-breasted young woman carrying a rifle, another chuckle: "One thing that has got to be dispelled is this myth of hopelessness. The myth that they can't win, so why support them . . . I wouldn't mind having her fighting alongside of me."

On such afternoons the enemy was manifold, and often within. The "Red Empire" was of course the enemy. "Christian communists" were also the enemy. "Guilt-ridden masochistic liberals" were the enemy, and "the radical chic crowd that always roots for the other side," the "Beverly Hills liberals with their virulent hatred of America." I recall a briefing on the 1984 Salvadoran election in which "people like Tom Brokaw" were the enemy, people like Richard Meislin of *The New York Times* and Sam Dillon of the *Miami Herald*, people whose "sneer was showing," people who "did not need to be in El Salvador to write what they did"; people who were "treated well" (". . . although the bar at the Camino Real was closed for the day, they got back to it that night . . .") but persisted in following what the briefer of the day, a frequent speaker named Daniel James, who had been in the 1950s managing editor of *The New Leader* and whose distinctly polemical interest in Latin America had led him to the directorship of the Americas Coalition, one of several amorphous groups formed to support the administration's Central American policy, referred to as "the media party line."

"I'm saying 'party line' in quotes," Daniel James had added quickly. "Because I don't mean to imply that there's any kind of political party involved." This kind of parenthetical disclaimer was not uncommon in Room 450, where irony, or "saying in quotes," was often signaled by raising two fingers on each hand and wiggling them. "Party line" was in quotes, yet there were for Daniel James "just too many similarities" in stories filed from El Salvador. The American press, it seemed, had been "making up deeds of right-wing terror" in El Salvador. The American press, it seemed, had been refusing to "put tough questions to the guerrillas" in El Salvador. "What does that tell you?" Daniel James had asked that afternoon in 1984. "Is this responsible reporting? Or is it done with some kind of political motivation?"

The answer to such questions was, in Room 450, understood, since the meetings of the White House Outreach Working Group on Central America were attended almost exclusively by what might have seemed the already converted, by the convinced, by administration officials and by exiles from the countries in question and by native ideologues from both the heart and the distant fringes of the American Right; true believers who in many cases not only attended the briefings but on occasion gave them. I recall seeing Sam Dickens of the American Security Council, which had co-sponsored the lunch and press conference at which Roberto D'Aubuisson spoke during his illegal 1980 visit to Washington and which was already deeply committed to aiding the Nicaraguan contras. I recall seeing Lynn Francis Bouchey, one of the authors of the Santa Fe document and the chairman of the Council for Inter-American Security, which was equally committed. "Hear, hear," Lynn Francis Bouchey said when Jack Wheeler asked him if the situation in Mozambique did not remind him of the situation in Nicaragua.

This was not a group which would have appeared to need much instruction in administration policy in Central America. This was not a group apt to raise those questions about Central America commonly raised in less special venues. In fact there was for many people in Room 450 just one question about Central America, which was why the United States was compelled to deal through surrogates there when it could be fighting its own war for the minds of mankind, and it was this question that the briefers addressed by tapping into the familiar refrain: the United States was forced to deal through surrogates because of the defeatists, because of the appeasers, because of the cowards and the useful fools and the traitors, because of what Jack Wheeler had called "that virulent hatred for America as a culture and as a nation and as a society" which was understood, by virtually everyone in the room, to infect the Congress, to infect the State Department, and above all to infect the media, which were, as Otto Juan Reich had said not long after he was appointed coordinator of public diplomacy, "being played like a violin by the Sandinistas."

There were some tricky points in this, although none that the briefers did not negotiate to the apparent satisfaction of most people in the room. The United States was forced to wage the war for the minds of mankind (or, as J. William Middendorf, U.S. ambassador to the OAS, was calling it, "the battle for the freedom of the western world") through surrogates, but in any case these surrogates could, if allowed to do so, win: "The only thing keeping the contras from victory is Congress," as Alexander M. Haig, Jr., had advised the group in Room 450. The war for the minds of mankind was being fought through surrogates only because the United States was thwarted in its wish to enter the war directly, but in any case the entry of the United States could not affect the outcome: "What is needed to shatter the myth of the inevitability of Marxist-Leninism is a genuine peasant rebellion from within a Soviet colony," as Jack Wheeler had advised the group in Room 450. "These heroic freedom fighters ask only for our help, they do not want us to fight for them."

An arresting amount of administration effort went into what might have seemed this marginal project. The weekly planning meetings for the Outreach program were attended not only by Faith Ryan Whittlesey and her aides at the Office of Public Liaison but also by representatives from the United States Information Agency, from the Central Intelligence Agency, from the State Department and from the National Security Council. The National Security Council was often represented by the protean Colonel Oliver North (Colonel North was responsible as well for overseeing Otto Juan Reich's Office of Public Diplomacy at the State Department), who was, according to a *Washington Post* story in August of 1985, a "mainstay" of the Outreach project, not only in the planning meetings but also as a "briefer of choice" in Room 450 itself.

Some of the peculiarity inherent in the Outreach project seemed clear enough at the time. It was of course clear that the program had been designed principally, if not entirely, as a weekly audience between the administration and its most passionate, most potentially schismatic communicants; a bone thrown to those famously restless troops on the far frontiers of the faith. It was also clear that many people in Room 450 on these Wednesday afternoons had links to, or could be useful to, the private funding network then being quite publicly organized, in support of the Reagan Doctrine and the war for the minds of mankind, under the official direction of Major General John K. Singlaub and what was known even then to be the unofficial direction of some of the very administration officials who gave the briefings in Room 450.

Other things were less clear than they might have been. One thing that was less clear, in those high years of the Reagan administration when we had not yet begun to see just how the markers were being moved, was how many questions there might later be about what had been the ends and what the means, what the problem and what the solution; about what, among people who measured the consequences of what they said and did exclusively in terms of approval ratings affected and network news calibrated and pieces of legislation passed or not passed, had come first, the war for the minds of mankind or the private funding network or the need to make a move for those troops on the far frontiers. What was also less clear then, particularly in Washington, most abstract of cities, entirely absorbed by the messages it was sending itself, narcotized by its own action, rapt in the contemplation of its own markers and its own moves, was just how much residue was already on the board.

Steven Carr for example was residue. Jesus Garcia for example was residue. Steven Carr was, at twenty-six, a South Florida lowlife, a sometime Naples construction worker with the motto DEATH BEFORE DISHONOR and a flaming skull tattooed on his left biceps; a discharge from the Navy for alcohol abuse; and a grand-theft conviction for stealing two gold-and-diamond rings, valued at $578, given to his mother by his stepfather. "She only wore them on holidays, I thought she'd never notice they were gone," Steven Carr later said about the matter of his mother's rings. He did not speak Spanish. He had no interest in any side of the conflict in Nicaragua. Nonetheless, in March of 1985, according to the story he began telling after he had been arrested in Costa Rica on weapons charges and was awaiting trial at La Reforma prison in San José, Steven Carr had collected arms for the contras at various locations around Dade County, loaded them onto a chartered Convair 440 at Fort Lauderdale–Hollywood International Airport, accompanied this shipment to Ilopango airport in San Salvador, and witnessed the eventual delivery of the arms to a unit of 2506 veterans fighting with the contras from a base about three miles south of the Nicaraguan border.

This story later became familiar, but its significance at the time Steven Carr first told it, in the summer of 1985 to Juan Tamayo of the *Miami Herald*, was that he was the first person to publicly claim firsthand knowledge of all stages of a single shipment. By the summer of 1986, after Steven Carr had bonded out of La Reforma and was back in South Florida (the details of how he got there were disputed, but either did or did not involve American embassy officials in Panama and San José who either did or did not give him a plane ticket and instructions to "get the hell out of Dodge"), doing six months in the Collier County jail for violation of probation on the outstanding matter of his mother's rings, he was of course telling it as well to investigators from various congressional committees and from the U.S. attorney's office in Miami. This was the point, in August 1986, at which his lawyers asked that he be released early and placed, on the grounds that the story he was telling endangered his life, in a witness protection program. "I'm not too popular with a lot of people because I'm telling the truth," Steven Carr told the *Miami Herald* a few days before this petition was heard and denied. "I wouldn't feel very safe just walking the streets after all this is over."

Steven Carr was released from the Collier County jail, having served his full sentence, on November 20, 1986. Twenty-three days later, at two-thirty on the morning of December 13, 1986, Steven Carr collapsed outside the room he was renting in Panorama City, California (a room which, according to the woman from whom he had rented it, Jackie Scott, he rarely left, and in which he slept with the doors locked and the lights on), convulsed, and died, of an apparent cocaine overdose. "I'm sorry," Steven Carr had said when Jackie Scott, whose daughter had heard "a commotion" and woken her, found him lying in the driveway. Jackie Scott told the *Los Angeles Times* that she had not seen Steven Carr drinking or taking drugs that evening, nor could she shed any light on what he had said next: "I paranoided out—I ate it all."

Jesus Garcia was a former Dade County corrections officer who was, at the time he began telling his story early in 1986, doing time in Miami for illegal possession of a MAC-10 with silencer. Jesus Garcia, who had been born in the United States of Cuban parents and thought of himself as a patriot, talked about having collected arms for the contras during the spring of 1985, and also about the plan, which he said had been discussed in the cocktail lounge of the Howard Johnson's near the Miami airport in February of 1985, to assassinate the new American ambassador to Costa Rica, blow up the embassy there, and blame it on the Sandinistas. The idea, Jesus Garcia said, had been to give the United States the opportunity it needed to invade Nicaragua, and also to collect on a million-dollar contract the Colombian cocaine cartel was said to have out on the new American ambassador to Costa Rica, who had recently been the American ambassador to Colombia and had frequently spoken of what he called "narco-guerrillas."

There were in the story told by Jesus Garcia and in the story told by Steven Carr certain details that appeared to coincide. Both Jesus Garcia and Steven Carr mentioned the Howard Johnson's near the Miami airport, which happened also to be the Howard Johnson's with the seventeen-dollar-a-night "guerrilla discount." Both Jesus Garcia and Steven Carr mentioned meetings in Miami with an American named Bruce Jones, who was said to own a farm on the border between Costa Rica and Nicaragua. Both Jesus Garcia and Steven Carr mentioned Thomas Posey, the Alabama produce wholesaler who had founded the paramilitary group CMA, or Civilian Materiel Assistance, formerly Civilian Military Assistance. Both Jesus Garcia and Steven Carr mentioned Robert Owen, the young Stanford graduate who had gone to Washington to work on the staff of Senator Dan Quayle (R-Ind.), had then moved into public relations, at Gray and Company, had in January of 1985 founded the nonprofit Institute for Democracy, Education, and Assistance, or IDEA (which was by the fall of 1985 on a consultancy contract to the State Department's Nicaraguan Humanitarian Assistance Office), and had been, it was later revealed, carrying cash to and from Central America for Oliver North.

This was, as described, a small world, and one in which encounters seemed at once random and fated, as in the waking dream that was Miami itself. People in this world spoke of having "tripped into an organization." People saw freedom fighters on "Nightline," and then in Miami. People saw boxes in motel rooms, and concluded that the boxes contained C-4. People received telephone calls from strangers, and picked them up at the airport at three in the morning, and began looking for a private plane to fly to Central America. Some people just turned up out of the nowhere: Jesus Garcia happened to meet Thomas Posey because he was working the afternoon shift at the Dade

County jail on the day Thomas Posey was booked for trying to take a .380 automatic pistol through the X-ray machine on Concourse G at the Miami airport. Some people turned up not exactly out of the nowhere but all over the map: Jesus Garcia said that he had seen Robert Owen in Miami, more specifically, as an assistant U.S. attorney in Miami put it, "at that Howard Johnson's when they were planning that stuff," by which the assistant U.S. attorney meant weapons flights. Steven Carr said that he had seen Robert Owen in Costa Rica, witnessing a weapons delivery at the base near the Nicaraguan border. Robert Owen, when he eventually appeared before the select committees, acknowledged that he had been present when such a delivery was made, but said that he never saw the actual unloading, and that his presence on the scene was, as the *Miami Herald* put it, "merely coincidental": another random but fated encounter.

There were no particularly novel elements in either the story told by Jesus Garcia or the story told by Steven Carr. They were Miami stories, fragments of the underwater narrative, and as such they were of a genre familiar in this country since at least the Bay of Pigs. Such stories had often been, like these, intrinsically impossible to corroborate. Such stories had often been of doubtful provenance, had been either leaked by prosecutors unable to make a case or elicited, like these, in jailhouse interviews, a circumstance which has traditionally tended, like a DEATH BEFORE DISHONOR tattoo, to work against the credibility of the teller.

Any single Miami story, moreover, was hard to follow, and typically required a more extensive recall of other Miami stories than most people outside Miami could offer. Characters would frequently reappear. A convicted bomber named Hector Cornillot, a onetime member of Orlando Bosch's Cuban Power movement, turned out, for example, to have been during the spring of 1985 the night bookkeeper at the Howard Johnson's near the Miami airport. Motivation, often opaque in a first or a second appearance, might come clear only in a third, or a tenth.

Miami stories were low, and lurid, and so radically reliant on the inductive leap that they tended to attract advocates of an ideological or a paranoid bent, which was another reason they remained, for many people, easy to dismiss. Stories like these had been told to the Warren Commission in 1964, but many people had preferred to discuss what was then called the climate of violence, and the healing process. Stories like these had been told during the Watergate investigations in 1974, but the President had resigned, enabling the healing process, it was again said, to begin. Stories like these had been told to the Church committee in 1975 and 1976, and to the House Select Committee on Assassinations in 1977 and 1978, but many people had preferred to focus instead on the constitutional questions raised, not on the hypodermic syringe containing Black Leaf 40 with which the CIA was trying in November of 1963 to get Fidel Castro assassinated, not on Johnny Roselli in the oil drum in Biscayne Bay, not on that motel room in

Dallas where Marita Lorenz claimed she had seen the rifles and the scopes and Frank Sturgis and Orlando Bosch and Jack Ruby and the Novo brothers, but on the separation of powers, and the proper role of congressional oversight. "The search for conspiracy," Anthony Lewis had written in *The New York Times* in September of 1975, "only increases the elements of morbidity and paranoia and fantasy in this country. It romanticizes crimes that are terrible because of their lack of purpose. It obscures our necessary understanding, all of us, that in this life there is often tragedy without reason."

This was not at the time an uncommon note, nor was it later. Particularly in Washington, where the logical consequences of any administration's imperial yearnings were thought to be voided when the voting levels were next pulled, the study of the underwater narrative, these stories about what people in Miami may or may not have done on the basis of what people in Washington had or had not said, was believed to serve no useful purpose. That the assassination of John F. Kennedy might or might not have been the specific consequence of his administration's own incursions into the tropic of morbidity and paranoia and fantasy (as early as 1964, two staff attorneys for the Warren Commission, W. David Slawson and William Coleman, had prepared a memorandum urging the commission to investigate the possibility that Lee Harvey Oswald had been acting for, or had been set up by, anti-Castro Cuban exiles) did not recommend, in this view, a closer study of the tropic. That there might or

might not be, in the wreckage of the Reagan administration, certain consequences to that administration's
similar incursions recommended only, in this view,
that it was again time to focus on the mechanical
model, time to talk about runaway agencies, arrogance
in the executive branch, about constitutional crises and
the nature of the presidency, about faults in the structure, flaws in the process; time to talk, above all, about
1988, when the levers would again be pulled and the
consequences voided and any lingering morbidity dispelled by the enthusiasms, the energies, of the new
team. "Dick Goodwin was handling Latin America
and a dozen other problems," Arthur M. Schlesinger,
Jr., once told us about the early months of the Kennedy administration, as suggestive a sentence as has
perhaps been written about this tabula rasa effect in
Washington life.

In the late summer of 1985, some months after the
Outreach meeting in Room 450 of the Old Executive
Office Building in Washington at which I had heard
Jack Wheeler talk about the necessity for supporting
freedom fighters around the world, I happened to receive a letter ("Dear Fellow American") from Major
General John K. Singlaub, an invitation to the International Freedom Fighters Dinner to be held that September in the Crystal Ballroom of the Registry Hotel
in Dallas. This letter was dated August 7, 1985, a date
on which Steven Carr was already sitting in La Reforma prison in San José and on which Jesus Garcia
was one day short of receiving a call from a twenty-

nine-year-old stranger who identified himself as Allen Saum, who said that he was a major in the U.S. Marines and had been sent by the White House, who enlisted Jesus Garcia in a mission he described as "George Bush's baby," and who then telephoned the Miami office of the FBI and told them where they could pick up Jesus Garcia and his MAC-10. "He looked typical Ivy League, I thought he must be CIA," Jesus Garcia later said about "Allen Saum," who did not show up for Jesus Garcia's trial but did appear at a pretrial hearing, where he said that he took orders from a man he knew only as "Sam."

The letter from General Singlaub urged that any recipient unable to attend the Dallas dinner ($500 a plate) plan in any case to have his or her name listed on the International Freedom Fighters Commemorative Program ($50 a copy), which General Singlaub would, in turn, "personally present to President Reagan." Even the smallest donation, General Singlaub stressed, would go far toward keeping "freedom's light burning." The *mujaheddin* in Afghanistan, for example, who would be among the freedom fighters to benefit from the Dallas dinner (along with those in Angola, Laos, South Vietnam, Cambodia, Mozambique, Ethiopia, and of course Nicaragua), had not long before destroyed "approximately twenty-five per cent of the Afghan government's Soviet supplied air force" (or, according to General Singlaub, twenty MIGs, worth $100 million) with just "a few hundred dollars spent on plastic explosives."

I recall experiencing, as I read this sentence about

the *mujaheddin* and the few hundred dollars spent on plastic explosives, the exact sense of expanding, or contracting, possibility that I had recently experienced during flights to Miami. Many apparently disparate elements seemed to be converging in the letter from General Singlaub, and the convergence was not one which discouraged that "search for conspiracy" deplored by Anthony Lewis a decade before. The narrative in which a few hundred dollars spent on plastic explosives could reverse history, which appeared to be the scenario on which General Singlaub and many of the people I had seen in Room 450 were operating, was the same narrative in which meetings at private houses in Miami Beach had been seen to overturn governments. This was that narrative in which the actions of individuals had been seen to affect events directly, in which revolutions and counterrevolutions had been framed in the private sector; that narrative in which the state security apparatus existed to be enlisted by one or another private player.

This was also the narrative in which words had tended to have consequences, and stories endings. NICARAGUA HOY, CUBA MAÑANA. When Jesus Garcia talked about meeting in the cocktail lounge of the Howard Johnson's near the Miami airport to discuss a plan to assassinate the American ambassador to Costa Rica, bomb the American embassy there, and blame it on the Sandinistas, the American ambassador he was talking about was Lewis Tambs, one of the authors of the Santa Fe document, the fifty-three pages which had articulated for many people in Washington the reasons for the exact American involvement in the politics of the Caribbean which this plan discussed in the cocktail lounge of the Howard Johnson's near the Miami airport was meant to ensure. Let me tell you about Cuban terrorists, Raúl Rodríguez had said at the midnight dinner in the Arquitectonica condominium overlooking Biscayne Bay. Cuba never grew plastique. Cuba grew tobacco, Cuba grew sugarcane. Cuba never grew C-4.

The air that evening in Miami had been warm and soft even at midnight, and the glass doors had been open onto the terrace overlooking the bay. The daughter of the fifteenth president of the Republic of Cuba, María Elena Prío Durán, whose father's grave at Woodlawn Park Cemetery in Miami lay within sight of the private crypt to which the body of another exiled president, Anastasio Somoza Debayle of Nicaragua, was flown forty-eight hours after his assassination in Asunción (no name on this crypt, no dates, no epitaph, only the monogram "AS" worked among the lilies on a stained-glass window, as if the occupant had negotiated himself out of history), had lit her cigarette and immediately put it out. When Raúl Rodríguez said that evening that C-4 grew here, he was talking about what it had cost to forget that decisions made in Washington had effects outside Washington; about the reverberative effect of certain ideas, and about their consequences. This dinner in Miami took place on March 26, 1985. The meetings in Miami described by Jesus Garcia had already taken place. The flights out of Miami described by Jesus Garcia and

Steven Carr had already taken place. These meetings and these flights were the least of what had already taken place; of what was to take place; and also of what, in this world where stories have tended to have endings, has yet to take place. "As a matter of fact I was very definitely involved in the decisions about support to the freedom fighters," the fortieth President of the United States said more than two years later, on May 15, 1987. "My idea to begin with."

NOTES

These notes are meant only as a guide, and reflect only the smallest part of those published sources on which I have drawn and to whose authors I owe thanks. Aside from published sources, I would like particularly to thank, among the many people who were helpful to me in Miami and in Washington, the editors and staff of the Miami Herald, *especially Madeleine Blais and John Katzenbach; Frank Calzón at the Cuban American National Foundation; Ernesto Betancourt at Radio Martí; Carlos Luis at the Museo Cubano de Arte y Cultura in Miami; Ricardo Pau-Llosa at Miami-Dade Community College in Miami; and Mr. and Mrs. George Stevens, Jr., in Washington. I would like also to thank, in New York, Robert Silvers, Michael Korda, Lois Wallace, Sophie Sorkin, and especially Rebecca Stowe, whose tireless willingness to research even the smallest point has made any error in this book entirely my own.*

CHAPTER 1, *pages 11 to 20*

I am indebted for much of the historical detail in this chapter to Hugh Thomas, *Cuba* (London: Eyre & Spottiswoode, 1971). The photograph of the Prío family leaving Havana appeared in *Cuba*, and before that in *Life*, March 24, 1952.

"They say that I was a terrible president . . .": *A Thousand Days* by Arthur M. Schlesinger, Jr. (Boston: Houghton Mifflin, 1965), p. 216.

An account of the attempt to land a third force in

Camagüey Province appears in *The Winds of December* by John Dorschner and Roberto Fabricio (New York: Coward, McCann & Geoghegan, 1980). Dorschner and Fabricio also provide a detailed account of Fulgencio Batista's departure from Havana on January 1, 1959.

The Kennedy campaign statement mentioned on page 19 is discussed by Schlesinger in *A Thousand Days*, p. 72.

The Nicaraguan Refugee Fund dinner at which Ronald Reagan spoke was covered by both the *Miami Herald* and *The New York Times* on April 16, 1985.

CHAPTER 2, *pages 23 to 29*

The *Miami Herald* report mentioning "guerrilla discounts" was by Juan Tamayo and appeared July 21, 1985, under the headline, "Cuban exiles said to ship guns to rebels."

The pamphlet giving tips for maintaining a secure profile was reported by Brian Duffy in the *Miami Herald*, June 5, 1985, under the headine, "Smuggling guidebook offers 'how to' hints."

"Well-heeled investors returning north" appeared in the *Herald* on June 16, 1985. "Costly condos threatened with massive foreclosures" appeared August 2, 1985, and "Foreclosures soaring in S. Florida" on March 28, 1986. "Arena financing plan relies on hotel guests" appeared June 7, 1985, and "S. Florida hotel rooms get emptier" on October 19, 1985. The real-estate analyst quoted on page 28 was Mike Cannon, president of Appraisal and Real Estate Economics Associates, Inc., quoted by Dory Owens in "Wirth betting that office glut will end," *Miami Herald*, July 17, 1985.

Reports on Theodore Gould and Miami Center appeared in the *Miami Herald* on August 9 and October 11, 1985.

CHAPTER 3, *pages 30 to 38*

Reports by Brian Duffy and Nancy Ancrum on the cache of hand grenades and the pawnbroker appeared in the *Miami Herald* on October 25 and November 2, 1985. Debbie Sontag's report ("Former guard accidentally kills self in Beach supermarket lot") on the shooting in the Miami Beach parking lot appeared October 9, 1985. The arrest of Jose "Coca Cola" Yero was reported by Jeff Leen in the October 22, 1985, *Herald*. Charisse L. Grant's report on the young woman who was car-bombed in South Palm Beach ("Bomb victim feared for her life, cops say") appeared June 28, 1986.

CHAPTER 4, *pages 39 to 48*

Black tensions in Miami have been extensively covered since 1980 not only in the *Herald* but in *The New York Times* and the *Los Angeles Times*. For background see *The Miami Riot of 1980* by Bruce Porter and Marvin Dunn (Lexington, Mass.: D. C. Heath and Company—Lexington Books, 1984); "Overwhelmed in Miami" by John Katzenbach in *Police Magazine*, September 1980; "Under Siege in an Urban Ghetto" by Bruce Porter and Marvin Dunn in *Police Magazine*, July 1981; and "Open Wounds" by Madeleine Blais in the *Miami Herald*'s Sunday magazine, *Tropic*, May 12, 1985.

The quote from the president of the Orange Bowl committee appeared in "CRB 'slaps' OB for party at restrictive club," by Marc Fisher, *Miami Herald*, March 21, 1985. Membership policies at South Florida private clubs were covered in Marc Fisher's three-part report on private clubs, appearing in the *Herald* on April 7, 8, and 9, 1985. The Surf Club party on page 45 was mentioned in "Miami's Elite Holds Fast to Tradition," April 4, 1985, part of a *Herald* series on "Society in South Florida."

For background on Mariel, see *The Cuban-American Experience: Culture, Images and Perspectives* by

Thomas D. Boswell and James R. Curtis (Totowa, N.J.: Rowman & Allanheld, 1984); *Cuban Americans: Masters of Survival* by José Llanes (Cambridge, Mass.: Abt Books, 1982); and "The Cubans: A People Divided" and "The Cubans: A People Changed," two *Miami Herald* Special Reports published as supplements to the editions of December 11 and 18, 1983. This chapter also draws on a 1985 study by Helga Silva called "Children of Mariel: From Shock to Integration," provided to me by the Cuban American National Foundation in Washington, D.C.

CHAPTER 5, *pages 49 to 62*

"The Most Influential People in Dade's History" and "The Most Important Events in Dade's History" appeared in the *Miami Herald*, February 3, 1986. The population statistics on page 51 are those given for 1986 by the Miami Chamber of Commerce.

The *Herald* reports on "Cuban Miami: A Guide for Non-Cubans" appeared each Friday from October 10 to November 21, 1986. The *Herald* piece in which Luis Botifoll was quoted was by Guillermo Martinez and appeared in *Tropic* on January 16, 1983. The *Herald* food section mentioned was that for March 20, 1986. A note on the Miami Springs Holiday Inn and its 26 Julio bar special appeared in Fred Tasker's *Herald* column on July 26, 1985.

The address quoted by Vice President George Bush was delivered in Miami on May 20, 1986.

The column by George Will ("The First Contras") appeared in *Newsweek*, March 31, 1986. George Gilder's piece ("Making It") appeared in the Winter 1985 issue of *The Wilson Quarterly*. The "samba" report on the Calle Ocho Festival appeared in the *Herald*, March 10, 1986.

CHAPTER 6, *pages 63 to 67*

The lines quoted are from p. 34 of the transcript for a January 19, 1984, meeting of the Miami City Commission, and the speaker was Maurice Ferre, then mayor of Miami.

Robert Melby was quoted in the *Miami Herald*, March 21, 1985, in a report ("English proponent renews drive") by Andres Viglucci. The reference to Xavier Suarez's "flawless English" appeared in the *Los Angeles Times*, November 13, 1985, in a story ("Attorney Suarez Elected Mayor in Miami") credited to Times Wire Services. The *Herald* political editor quoted was Tom Fiedler, and the quoted lines appeared in his column ("On the fringes of politics"), October 6, 1985. The quoted note about Raul Masvidal's unlisted telephone number appeared in Fred Tasker's *Herald* column on September 23, 1985. The closing of Gator Kicks Longneck Saloon (which was, incidentally, the bar for whose advertising Donna Rice was photographed, before she met Gary Hart, with the Confederate flag) was covered in the *Herald* ("Colorful country roadhouse closes" by Ivonne Rovira Kelly), February 8, 1986. The quoted column by Charles Whited appeared February 9, 1986.

CHAPTER 7, *pages 68 to 80*

Jim Hampton's column ("Voters' kiss of death? Kiss off!") appeared in the *Herald* November 17, 1985. The quotes from Andres Nazario Sargen and from police spokesmen on page 71 appeared in the *Herald*, March 21, 1986, in "Opposing rallies OKd at same site" by Andres Viglucci. The headlines and photograph mentioned on page 71 appeared March 23, 1986. Other sources on the Torch of Friendship demonstrations included "Suarez clarifies his stand on 'free speech'" by Justin Gillis, *Miami Herald*, April 5, 1986; the letters columns of the *Herald* for March 27 and 28, 1986 (a letter from Mayor

Suarez appeared March 27); Charles Whited's *Herald* column ("Impeding right to free speech is undemocratic") for March 25, 1986; and Carl Hiaasen's *Herald* column ("Goons who hit man at rally aren't patriots") for March 26, 1986.

The José Martí letter quoted on page 75 was to Manuel Mercado and appears in volume I of *Obras Completas*. The translation here is Hugh Thomas's.

The mayoralty candidate with the plan to confine minors to their houses was Evelio Estrella, and his statement appeared in the *Miami News* (in the "Miami Mayoral Forum" series) on October 10, 1985. General Benítez's statement appeared in the same series October 8, 1985.

"Resort sells sun, fun—in Cuba" by Alfonso Chardy appeared in the *Herald*, April 17, 1985. "Free markets allow Havana to spiff up," also by Alfonso Chardy (whose ethnic background remained a source of some speculation in the Cuban community), appeared March 25, 1985.

The José Martí lines on page 79 are from volume III of *Obras Completas*, and also appear on p. 109 of *José Martí: Thoughts/Pensamientos* (New York: Eliseo Torres & Sons—Las Américas Publishing Co., 1980 and 1985), by Carlos Ripoll, whose translation this is.

For the Kennedy and Reagan quotes see notes on chapter 1.

CHAPTER 8, *pages 83 to 98*

Allen Dulles is quoted by Schlesinger in *A Thousand Days*, p. 242; John F. Kennedy on p. 257.

The poll mentioned on p. 84 appeared in *Tropic*, *Miami Herald*, January 16, 1983. The existence of The Non-Group was first reported by Celia W. Dugger in "The 38 who secretly guide Dade," *Miami Herald*, September 1, 1985.

The Theodore C. Sorensen quotes on pages 86 and 89

appear in his *Kennedy* (New York: Harper & Row, 1965), p. 722.

For background on JM/WAVE, see William R. Amlong, "How the CIA operated in Dade," *Miami Herald*, March 9, 1975; Taylor Branch and George Crile III, "The Kennedy Vendetta," *Harper's*, August 1975; *Portrait of a Cold Warrior* by Joseph Burkholder Smith (New York: G. P. Putnam's Sons, 1976); and *Investigation of the Assassination of President John F. Kennedy: Hearings before the Select Committee on Assassinations of the U.S. House of Representatives, 95th Congress* (Washington, D.C.: U.S. Government Printing Office, 1979), particularly volume X. CIA activities out of Miami during this period are also discussed in *The Investigation of the Assassination of President John F. Kennedy: Performance of the Intelligence Agencies*, which is book V of the *Final Report of the Select Committee to Study Governmental Operations with respect to Intelligence Activities, U.S. Senate, 94th Congress* (Washington, D.C.: U.S. Government Printing Office, 1976).

The December 1962 appearance of President and Mrs. Kennedy at the Orange Bowl is discussed by Sorensen in *Kennedy*, p. 308, and by Schlesinger in both *A Thousand Days*, p. 839, and *Robert Kennedy and His Times* (New York: Ballantine Books, 1979), p. 579. "But had CIA been up to its old tricks?" appears in *Robert Kennedy and His Times*, p. 586.

The financing of Southern Air Transport was reported by William R. Amlong in "CIA sold airline cheap," *Miami Herald*, March 10, 1975, and also by Martin Merzer in "Airline does job—quietly," *Miami Herald*, December 10, 1986.

The Schlesinger quotes on page 93 are from *Robert Kennedy and His Times*, p. 588. The Church committee testimony quoted on page 93 was given on May 16, 1976, and quoted on p. 11 of book V, *The Investigation of the Assassination of President John F. Kennedy: Performance of the Intelligence Agencies*.

There is a section on JURE, and on "autonomous operations," beginning on p. 77 of volume X of the 1979 *Investigation of the Assassination of President John F. Kennedy: Hearings before the Select Committee on Assassinations of the U.S. House of Representatives.* There is an account of the June 1963 Special Group meeting authorizing CIA supervision of exile actions within Cuba in the Church committee's 1975 *Interim Report: Alleged Assassination Plots Involving Foreign Leaders.*

The CIA internal report quoted appears on p. 126 of volume IV of the 1979 *Investigation of the Assassination of President John F. Kennedy: Hearings before the Select Committee on Assassinations of the U.S. House of Representatives.*

The Schlesinger quote on page 96 appears on p. 586 of *Robert Kennedy and His Times.* The Kennedy quote appears on p. 14 of volume X of the 1979 *Investigation of the Assassination of President John F. Kennedy: Hearings before the Select Committee on Assassinations of the U.S. House of Representatives.* James Angleton was quoted by Dick Russell, after a series of interviews which took place at the Army-Navy Club in Washington, in "Little Havana's Reign of Terror," *New Times,* October 29, 1976.

The footnote from *Robert Kennedy and His Times* appears on p. 513. The testimony before the Church committee mentioned on page 97 was given May 6, 1976, and quoted on p. 14, book V, *Final Report of the U.S. Senate Select Committee to Study Governmental Operations with respect to Intelligence Activities.*

The Kennedy quote on p. 97 appears in *A Thousand Days,* p. 839. The Sorensen quote appears in *Kennedy,* p. 722. The Schlesinger quote appears in *Robert Kennedy and His Times,* p. 579.

CHAPTER 9, *pages 99 to 108*

A report on the arrest of Eduardo Arocena ("Arocena 'Armory' Uncovered" by Jim McGee) appeared in the *Miami Herald*, July 24, 1983, and the quotes from Miriam Arocena, from the head of the 2506, from Andres Nazario Sargen, and from Tomas Garcia Fuste, the news director of WQBA, appeared in this piece. For Xavier Suarez and the Arocena defense fund, see Helga Silva and Guy Gugliotta, " 'La Causa' binds exile community," *Miami Herald* Special Report, December 11, 1983. Omega 7 itself has been covered since the late 1970s in both the *Herald* and *The New York Times*, which published a particularly complete report (" 'Highest Priority' Given by U.S. to Capture of Anti-Castro Group" by Robin Herman) on March 3, 1980.

For background on Max Lesnik, see Hugh Thomas, *Cuba;* John Dorschner and Roberto Fabricio, *The Winds of December;* and Helga Silva, "Those called 'soft' are often shunned," *Miami Herald* Special Report, December 11, 1983.

The incident with Luciano Nieves in the Versailles is mentioned by José Llanes in *Cuban Americans: Masters of Survival*, p. 127. According to the *Miami Herald* ("Killer asks for clemency," November 26, 1986), an exile named Valentin Hernandez was in 1978 convicted of the killing of Luciano Nieves and sentenced to twenty-five years without possibility of parole. Eight years later, when he petitioned the court for an early release, six thousand letters were received in support of his request, along with petitions describing him as "a political prisoner guilty of fighting against the oppression of communism."

CHAPTER 10, *pages 109 to 115*

The *diálogo*, and Orlando Padron and the cigar, are discussed by Barry Bearak, "Anti-Fidel Fervor Still Burns in Little Havana," *Los Angeles Times*, November 30, 1982. Also see David Vidal, "In Union City, the Memories of the Bay of Pigs Don't Die," *The New York Times*, December 21, 1979, and Jorge Fierro, "For the *Comunidad*, the Visit Is a Sad Show," *The New York Times*, January 20, 1980. Also: Max Azicri, "Un análisis pragmático del diálogo entre la Cuba del interior y la del exterior," *Areíto* IX, no. 36 (1984).

The quote from Fidel Castro appears on p. 67, *Diary of the Cuban Revolution* by Carlos Franqui (New York: The Viking Press, 1980).

For background on Carlos Muñiz Varela, see Luis Angel Torres, "Semblanza de Carlos Muñiz," *Areíto* IX, no. 36 (1984). The murder of Eulalio José Negrin was reported in *The New York Times*, November 26, 1979, "Cuban Refugee Leader Slain in Union City." The *El Diario-La Prensa* bombing was discussed by Robin Herman in the March 3, 1980, *New York Times* piece cited in the notes for Chapter 9. For the TWA bombing, see Robert D. McFadden, "Kennedy Bomb Hurts Four Workers in Baggage Area," *The New York Times*, March 26, 1979.

CHAPTER 11, *pages 116 to 125*

The translations of *Areíto*'s 1974 and 1984 statements of purpose are those provided by *Areíto*. The piece referring to exile Miami as "the deformed foetus . . ." appears in *Areíto* IX, no. 36 (1984) ("El Miami cubano" by Lourdes Argüelles and Gary MacEoin), and the translation is mine.

"Introduction to the Sandinista Documentary Cinema" (p. 118) appeared in *Areíto* X, no. 37 (1984). Marifeli Pérez-Stable was quoted by Helga Silva in "Those called soft . . . ," *Miami Herald* Special Report, December 11, 1983. For background on Lourdes Casal see *Areíto* IX, no. 36 (1984). Dolores Prida and the controversy over

Coser y Cantar were extensively covered in the *Miami Herald* during the first two weeks of May 1986.

The issue of *Areíto* referred to on page 121 is volume IX, no. 36, and the pieces referred to are "El Instituto de Estudios Cubanos o los estrechos límites del pluralismo" (Consejo de Dirección de Areíto) and "Sobre las relaciones entre el Instituto de Estudios Cubanos y Areíto: convergencias y divergencias" (María Cristina Herrera/ Consejo de Dirección de Areíto).

For the Unaccompanied Children's Program, see Michael J. McNally's *Catholicism in South Florida: 1868–1968* (Gainesville: University of Florida Press, 1982). The extracts from *Contra Viento y Marea* were reprinted in *Areíto* (vol. IX, no. 36), and the translation is mine.

CHAPTER 12, *pages 126 to 139*

For "the *P.M.* affair," see *Area Handbook for Cuba*, Foreign Area Studies of The American University (Washington, D.C.: U.S. Government Printing Office, 1976), p. 330; *Family Portrait with Fidel* by Carlos Franqui (New York: Vintage Books, 1985), pp. 131–33; and *A Man with a Camera* by Nestor Almendros (New York: Farrar, Straus & Giroux, 1984), p. 139. For *Bohemia*, see Franqui, *Family Portrait*, and also Hugh Thomas, *Cuba*, p. 1292.

About the Jorge Valls controversy: see Liz Balmaseda and Jay Ducassi, "Hero in jail, freed poet provokes exile ire," *Miami Herald*, September 2, 1984. About Armando Valladares: Carl Gershman, president of the National Endowment for Democracy, stated to the Senate Foreign Relations Committee on March 29, 1985, that Endowment efforts "in the fields of education, culture and communications" included "assistance to a program organized by the distinguished Cuban writer and former political prisoner Armando Valladares to inform European public opinion about the human rights situation in Cuba."

For background on Dr. Orlando Bosch, see pp. 89–93, volume X of the 1979 *Investigation of the Assassination of President John F. Kennedy: Hearings before the Select Committee* . . . , cited in the notes for Chapter 8. For background on Luis Posada Carriles, see Tim Golden, "Sandinistas say escapee ran supplies," *Miami Herald*, October 16, 1986; Sam Dillon, "Fugitive may be contra supplier," *Miami Herald*, October 21, 1986; Sam Dillon and Guy Gugliotta, "How jail escapee joined rebels' supply network," *Miami Herald*, November 2, 1986 (the spokesman for George Bush mentioned on page 136 is quoted in this report); and p. 44, volume X of the 1979 *Investigation of the Assassination of President John F. Kennedy* . . . , also cited for Chapter 8.

The president of the Committee to Free Orlando Bosch was quoted by Sandra Dibble, "Bosch's friends turn out to view exhibit of his artworks," *Miami Herald*, December 13, 1986. The letter in defense of Dr. Bosch appeared in *El Herald*, November 20, 1985; translation mine. Cosme Barros and Norma Garcia were quoted by Reinaldo Ramos, "To Miami Cubans, Bosch is folk hero," *Miami Herald*, July 27, 1986. The 1977 CIA document mentioned is discussed by Sam Dillon and Guy Gugliotta, "How jail escapee . . . ," cited above.

Orlando Bosch's CIA experience is discussed on p. 90, volume X of the 1979 *Investigation of the Assassination of President John F. Kennedy* . . . , cited above. The Richard Helms quote appears on p. 159 of volume IV, the same House Select Committee hearings.

CHAPTER 13, *pages 140 to 151*

Robert C. McFarlane was quoted by Joanne Omang in one of the first pieces to name Lieutenant Colonel Oliver North, "The White House's Nicaragua Middleman: A Marine Officer Implements Policy," *Washington Post National Weekly Edition*, August 26, 1985.

CHAPTER 14, *pages 152 to 163*

For Guillermo Novo and the Letelier case, see Taylor Branch and Eugene M. Propper, former assistant U.S. attorney for the District of Columbia, *Labyrinth* (New York: The Viking Press, 1982).

For Felipe Rivero and Cuban radio in Miami, see Fabiola Santiago, "When stations talk, listeners act" and "Some voices of Miami's Spanish-language radio," *Miami Herald*, June 22, 1986.

The Reagan radio talks about the death of Orlando Letelier are reprinted on pp. 521–23 of *On Reagan: The Man and His Presidency* by Ronnie Dugger (New York: McGraw-Hill, 1983). Jesse Helms was quoted by Taylor Branch and Eugene M. Propper in *Labyrinth*. Ronald Reagan on the blacklist was quoted by Robert Scheer on p. 259 of his *With Enough Shovels: Reagan, Bush & Nuclear War* (New York: Random House, 1982).

For Ronald Reagan on the Salvadoran death squads, see George Skelton, "Reagan Suspects Rebels of Death Squad Killings," *Los Angeles Times*, December 3, 1983. For Ronald Reagan on Sandinistas dressing up in freedom fighter uniforms, see "Nicaraguan killers really Sandinista agents," *Miami Herald*, March 16, 1986, and Rudy Abramson, "Sandinistas Kill in Contra Guise, Reagan Charges," *Los Angeles Times*, March 16, 1986.

Ronnie Dugger quotes David Gergen on pp. 463–64, *On Reagan*. For Ronald Reagan on "Medical science doctors confirm . . . ," see Francis X. Clines, "Reagan Tells Broadcasters Aborted Fetuses Suffer Pain," *The New York Times*, January 31, 1984. Hannah Arendt's discussion of propaganda appears on pp. 341–364 of *The Origins of Totalitarianism* (New York: Harcourt Brace, the 1966 edition).

For Ronald Reagan's 1983 visit to Miami see George Skelton, "Reagan Vows to Defend Latin American Liberty," *Los Angeles Times*, May 21, 1983; Reginald Stuart, "Cubans in Miami Await Reagan's Visit Eagerly," *The New York Times*, May 20, 1983, and Helga Silva and Liz

Balmaseda, "Superstar Wows Little Havana," *Miami Herald*, May 21, 1983.

CHAPTER 15, *pages 167 to 179*

"A couple of hours into our meeting . . .": see José Llanes, *Cuban Americans: Masters of Survival*, cited in the notes for Chapter 4, p. 74. "Our hearts sank . . ." and "I had never seen . . . ," see Schlesinger, *A Thousand Days*, pp. 283–284. For "rekindled doubts in Congress . . . ," see Philip Taubman, "Latin Debate Refocused," *New York Times*, April 9, 1984.

The Associated Press story quoting Larry Speakes and Michael Deaver (mentioned on page 174) was by Michael Putzel, and was on the wire April 12, 1984, for release April 15. David Gergen was quoted in *The New York Times* by Steven R. Weisman and Francis X. Clines in "Q. & A.: David R. Gergen—Key Presidential Buffer Looks Back," January 10, 1984. The quote from Morton Kondracke comes from his review of Robert Dallek's *Ronald Reagan: The Politics of Symbolism*, in *The New York Times Book Review*, March 4, 1984. The 1984 American Enterprise Institute discussion mentioned took place at the Mayflower Hotel in Washington on March 1, 1984, and was called "The Reagan Administration and the Press: What's the Problem?"

CHAPTER 16, *pages 180 to 208*

A New Inter-American Policy for the Eighties can be obtained in some libraries (Library of Congress Catalog Card No. 81–68443) or from the Council for Inter-American Security, 729 Eighth St., S.E., Washington, D.C. 20003. The Edward Cody piece mentioning the Santa Fe document is "Disappointment in Havana: No Thaw in U.S. Relations," *Washington Post National Weekly Edition*, June 17, 1985.

For the National Security Planning Group document mentioned on page 186, Project Truth, and the establishment of the Office of Public Diplomacy, see Alfonso Chardy, "Secrets leaked to harm Nicaragua, sources say," *Miami Herald*, October 13, 1986. Faith Ryan Whittlesey and Otto Juan Reich are quoted by Tim Golden, "Reagan Countering Critics of Policies in Central America," *Los Angeles Times*, December 21, 1983.

For background on Jack Wheeler, see Paul Dean, "Adventurer Devotes Energy to Anti-Communist Causes," *Los Angeles Times*, August 1, 1985. The *Washington Post* story mentioned on page 195 is Joanne Omang's "The White House's Nicaragua Middleman . . . ," cited in the notes for Chapter 13.

For background on Steven Carr and Jesus Garcia, see Juan Tamayo, "Cuban exiles said to ship guns to rebels," *Miami Herald*, July 21, 1985; Lori Rozsa, "Contra mercenary wants new life," *Miami Herald*, August 10, 1986; Steven J. Hedges, "Witness claimed U.S. aided escape," *Miami Herald*, January 6, 1987; Alfonso Chardy, "Contra weapons probe may bring first prosecution," *Miami Herald*, July 13, 1986; Lynn O'Shaughnessy and Mark Henry, "Witness in Nicaragua Arms Trafficking Dies," *Los Angeles Times*, December 15, 1986; Sandra Dibble, "Contra supporter lands in jail," *Miami Herald*, August 4, 1986; Stephen J. Hedges, "Independent counsel may end Miami probe," *Miami Herald*, December 30, 1986; Alfonso Chardy, "Rebel guns may spur U.S. probe," *Miami Herald*, July 12, 1986; "Inquiry Reported into Contra Arms," *The New York Times*, April 11, 1986; Caitlin Randall, "5 await trial in 'sensitive' Costa Rican case," *Miami Herald*, April 23, 1986; and, on Robert Owen: Alfonso Chardy, "Idealism drew him into contra struggle," *Miami Herald*, June 8, 1986, and Tim Golden, "State Department adviser tied to misuse of rebel aid," *Miami Herald*, February 16, 1987.

The column by Anthony Lewis mentioned on page 203, "What Not to Do," appeared in *The New York Times* September 25, 1975. The memorandum prepared by W. David Slawson and William Coleman is quoted at length on p. 5, volume X, of the 1979 *Investigation of the Assassination of President John F. Kennedy* . . . , cited in the notes for Chapter 8. The Schlesinger line quoted appears in *A Thousand Days*, p. 207.

INDEX